ALL MY LIFE A CIRCLE

Using the Tools: Circles, MAPS & PATHS

Mary A. Falvey
Marsha Forest
Jack Pearpoint
Richard L. Rosenberg

INCLUSION PRESS

Published by:
Inclusion Press ©
24 Thome Cres.
Toronto, Ontario
Canada M6H 2S5
Phone 416-658-5363   Fax 416-658-5067
e-mail: 74640.1124@compuserve.com
Web site: http://inclusion.com

Printed in
Toronto, Canada
at New Concept

Proceeds from sales will assist the

*Centre for Integrated
Education and Community*

Canadian Cataloguing in Publication Data

Falvey, Mary, 1950-
Forest, Marsha, 1942-
Pearpoint, Jack, 1945-
Rosenberg, Richard, 1954-

Main entry under title:

All my life's a circle:
using the tools: circles, MAPS & PATH

New expanded edition
Includes bibliographical references and index.
ISBN   1-895418-26-7

1. Social Integration. 2. Handicapped.
I. Falvey, Mary A., 1950-

HV1568.A64 1997   362.4   C97-932163-8

All My Life's A Circle

All my life's a circle,
sunrise & sundown
The Moon rolls thru the night-time
'til the daybreak comes around.

All my life's a circle,
but I can't tell you why.
Seasons spinning round again;
the years keep rolling by.

It seems like I've been here before;
I can't remember when;
but I got this funny feeling
that we'll all be together again.

There's no straight lines make up my life
and all my roads have bends.
There's no clear cut beginnings
& so far, no dead ends.

Well, I've found you a thousand times;
I guess you've done the same.
But then we lose each other;
It's just like a children's game.

But as I find you here again,
the thought runs thru my mind:
Our love is like a circle;
let's go round one more time.

All my life's a circle,
sunrise & sundown.
The Moon rolls thru the night-time
'til the daybreak comes around.

Harry Chapin

Prince Ipal's Story

Once upon a time, in a land far away, there lived a regular education teacher. Now this teacher was very comfortable in his surroundings, as were most regular education teachers. You see, in the land, called *Exclusive Education*, regular education teachers taught regular kids, and there was peace across the land. But one day, in late August, this particular regular education teacher was told that he was to have two irregular students. They were called *"students with severe challenges,"* but this teacher knew that if they weren't regular kids, they, logically, must be irregular. This frightened the teacher, so he went to the Prince of the land, Prince-Ipal, and complained.

"These children won't fit into my regular education class," the teacher cried, *"surely there must be a place somewhere in your great Kingdom to put them where they all fit in."*

"Alas, there is nothing I can do," replied Prince-Ipal, *"for the King has declared that the land shall be renamed. The knew name for our Kingdom shall be 'Inclusion'."*

"But Sire," complained the teacher, *"Surely there will be an uprising among all the subjects in the Kingdom. After all, we have a special education classroom that has such a light load, and my load is so heavy. If I wanted to be a special education teacher, I would have gone into special education. What do I do with them? How about the rest of the kids in the class? Who will keep my hair from turning grey?"*

"I have told you that I can do nothing," said Prince-Ipal. *"Be gone now, and beg me no more, for I can not do as you wish."*

And so the teacher sought out the wise old sage, known as the inclusion teacher, for she was known to have magical powers.

"Wise Old Sage," said the teacher, *"what am I to do? You have a special education classroom, how can you refuse to take these students with severe challenges when your load is so light and mine so heavy? Surely you must know that they would fit in much better with you than with me!"*

But the Wise Old Sage did not reply to the question that the teacher had asked, and said simply, *"Seek, and you shall find the answers to all of the questions that are in your mind."*

"Damn," replied the teacher, for he was not used to such frustration in his comfortable regular education position.

But the wise old sage remained unshaken. *"Seek out workshops, and ask the children, for this is your destiny, and you shall not fail. I do not have magical powers, but remember that I will support you, and provide for you what I can. Your King has decreed that all children can learn, and this I know to be true. Now go in search of knowledge."*

And go he did. And he learned that through collaborative teaming, cooperative learning, partial participation, matrixing IEP objectives, community support, asking the children, and treating all children like children, that the new Kingdom called *Inclusion* would work, and would continue to work. The teacher also saw a remarkable thing happen: he saw that regular education teachers and special education teachers started to become just teachers, and regular kids and special kids started to become just kids. And the teacher could see that soon there would once again be peace across the land. And the subjects of the *Kingdom of Inclusion* would live happily ever after.

The End

Clint Jones

Dedication

This book is dedicated to the continuation
of the work and spirit of two wonderful friends:

Sheila Jupp
who was tragically killed on May 2, 1994

Shafik Asante
who died Sept. 5, 1997

All My Life's a Circle

Contents

All My Life's a Circle 1

CIRCLE OF SUPPORT (FRIENDS) 5

MAKING ACTION PLANS (MAPS) 15
Where to begin 18

Question #1: What's a MAP? 19
Question #2: What is person's history or story? 20
Question #3: What are your dreams? 21
Question #4: What are your nightmares? 24
Question #5: Who is the person? 25
Question #6: What are the person's strengths, gifts, and talents? 26
Question #7: What does the person need? 27
Question #8: What is the plan of action? 28

PATH 31
Step 1 - The North Star - the Dream 33
Step 2 - The Goal 34
Step 3 - Now 35
Step 4 - Who Do We Enroll? 36
Step 5 - Getting Stronger 37
Step 6   - 3 Months 38
Step 7- 1 Month 39
Step 8 - The First Step (s) 40
CONSIDERATIONS/ CAUTIONS 41
SUMMARY 43

Recommended Viewing and Reading: 46

References 48

NEW ADDITIONS

SHAFIK'S MAP - the Video Transcript 50

JUDITH SNOW ON DREAMING 64

COLLECTED ARTICLES

Inclusion Is Not Exclusion 67

What is Person Centered Planning? 68

Introductory MAPS/PATH Learning Checklist 69

MAPS and PATH - Differences & Similarities 70

What is Inclusion? 71

There are No Disabled People 72

Joel and Bryce: A Lesson in Friendship 74

Listen to the Children: Hope was Ignited 84

Circles, MAPS and PATH: Creative Tools for Change 87

Life is Either a Daring Adventure, or Nothing at All! 90

Putting ALL Kids on the MAP 105

All My Life's a Circle

He aha te mea nui i tenei ao
maku e ki atu
He tangata! He tangata! He tangata!

Ask me what is most important in this world
Let me tell you.
It is people! It is people! It is people!
Maori Proverb

Schools that model and reflect the values of including all their students are those that are systematically building connec tions between the school and the school community partici-pants. Building such community connections are essential in order to foster a sense of belonging to the school community (O'Brien & Mount, 1991, Strully & Strully, 1985). These community connections and friendships are critical for many reasons. In order to avoid loneliness; in order to develop social, communicative, and even cognitive skills; in order to feel like a valued member of the community; and in order to develop the support needed to co-exist in a community are just a few of the reasons for building community connections and friendships (Stainback & Stainback, 1990; and Stainback, Stainback, & Wilkinson, 1992).

One of the key characteristics of building connections and friendships is that people have close proximity and frequent opportunities to interact with each other (Asher, Odem, & Gottman, 1977; Hartup, 1975; Howes, 1983; Lewis & Rosenblaum, 1975). This research has demonstrated that in order for children and adults to form the necessary bonds for friendships, they must have frequent access to one another. This access is facilitated when students are regularly in close proximity to one another. So it follows that students who attend the same school as the other students who live in their neighborhood are more likely to form bonds that are strong enough to result in friendship (Grenot-Scheyer, Coots, & Falvey, 1989).

The real voyage of discovery consists not in seeking new landscapes but in having new eyes.
Marcel Proust

Traditionally, special educators have been training and teaching students to be independent. Recently, emphasis has been placed on Interdependence (O'Brien & Mount 1991; Condeluci, 1991). Interdependence is the ability to connect with individuals with in ones own community and develop a network of supports to assist in accomplishing life goals.

There are too many unhappy, unloving, untrusting, and just mediocre schools. These schools do not teach nor do they emulate such principles as love, passion, openness and the love for learning. The academic subjects are important only if they are used to teach these principles, as illustrated in a very powerful way by Ginott (1972) in his **Letter to Teachers:**

Dear Teacher,

**I am a survivor of a concentration camp.
My eyes saw what no man
should witness.**

**Gas chambers built by
learned engineers.
Children poisoned by
educated physicians.
Infants killed by trained nurses.
Women & babies shot & burned
by high school &
college graduates.**

So I am suspicious of education.

**My request is that teachers help
students become human.
Your efforts must never produce
learned monsters,
skilled psychopaths,
educated Eichmanns.**

**Reading, writing, arithmetic are important
only
if they serve to make our children
more human.**

Teachers burn out in schools and classrooms that are teaching basic core academic skills out of the context of teaching values. Schools must be places where students are taught such skills as creating a just community and society, and caring for and helping one another.

Louise and Her Friends

For five years, a group of teenagers fought a high school district in a western state who refused to allow one of their peers, Louise, to enter or attend the same high school as the rest of them. The high school district claimed that because of her diabetes and other severe cognitive and physical disability labels, she had to attend a special education segregated class in a different high school. Since Louise was in seventh grade, she had attended the same school and classes as her peers.

When the high school district forced Louise to attend a different high school her friends were outraged. They had learned about the United States Constitution in their eighth grade Civics class, and felt that by denying Louise access to her neighborhood high school, her rights and their rights were being violated. They launched a campaign seeking support from advocates and their community. Their plight and their struggle were frequently written about in the newspaper; they appeared on local television news programs; and they presented to local governmental and advocacy groups, including the local city council and the board of education. In addition, they wrote and performed a "rap" song entitled "Friends" which tells their story, what they wanted and why. In April, 1993, the students' struggle was over, the school district reversed its decision and granted Louise the opportunity to attend the same school and classes as her peers and friends. What is so compelling about this true story, is that the students, Louise and her circle of friends, formed their relationship and subsequent friendships based upon their opportunity to go to school and classes together while in junior high school. There were no adults who told the students to care about Louise because she was "special", or to treat her different because she had diabetes and/or severe disability labels. Going to school and classes together gave these students the opportunity to know each other and become friends, they just wanted that opportunity back.

Whatever you can do or dream...
Begin it.
Boldness has the power and magic in it.
    Goethe

3

What this true story dramatizes is the need that children naturally feel to develop friendships. This natural phenomenon would continue if policy makers and educators just gave all students a chance. Unfortunately, frequent opportunities and close proximity are not always enough in order for children and adolescents to feel connected and build a network of friends. Several tools have been used to successfully facilitate such connections and eventual friendships. These tools are designed to tap into the creative energy of students and educators. The Circle of Friends is the foundation, followed by Making Action Plans (MAPs) and then Planning Alternatives Tomorrows with Hope (PATH). All three of these tools are person centered and assume the capacity theory where everyone is valued. They are based on hope for the future and begin with the assumptions that all people belong, all can learn, we are better off together, and diversity is one of our most critical strengths. These tools, Circles of Friends, MAPs, and PATH will be described in detail in the remainder of this booklet.

CIRCLE OF SUPPORT (FRIENDS)

A circle of friends is something that many of us take for granted unless we do not have one. A circle of friends provides us with a network of support of family and friends. A circle of friends is available when one needs someone to listen, to give loving advice, and to provide support when it is needed (Perske, 1989). In the absence of a naturally formed circle of friends, educators can facilitate a circle process, which can be used to enlist the involvement and commitment of peers around an individual student. For a student who is not well connected or does not have an extensive network of friends, the circle of friends process can be useful.

Friends do not live in harmony merely, but in melody.
     Thoreau

A circle of friends involves gathering together a group of students for the purpose of discovering their own networks and then reflecting on each others circles (Sherwood, 1990). Figure 1 provides a list of the steps involved in conducting a circle of friends process.

Often adults prefer to call this tool the circle of support, but children and teenagers we have talked to clearly have told us they like the term Circle of Friends.

CIRCLE OF SUPPORT (FRIENDS)

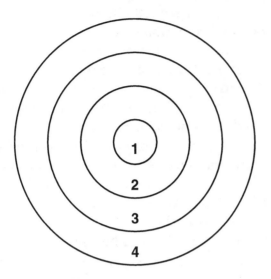

First Circle: *Circle of INTIMACY*

Second Circle: *Circle of FRIENDSHIP*

Third Circle: *Circle of PARTICIPATION*

Fourth Circle: *Circle of EXCHANGE*

Fill Circles from the Outside—In!

This exercise is a social scan. It will give a quick picture of who is in your life. It is very useful to gain clarity about who might be involved in certain activities, or circles that need to be filled. We recommend it personally and consider it an essential preventive health check for students, teachers and citizens. The hidden key question is: *"Who loves this person?"*

Instructions:
• *Draw four concentric circles.*
• *Put yourself in the middle then take a few minutes to fill in the people in each of your four circles.*

> • **FIRST Circle: The Circle of INTIMACY**
> *List the people most intimate in your life – those you cannot imagine living without.*
>
> • **SECOND Circle: The Circle of FRIENDSHIP**
> *List good friends – those who almost made the first circle.*
>
> • **THIRD Circle: The Circle of PARTICIPATION**
> *List people, organizations, networks you are involved with (work colleagues, the choir, the square dance club, your soft ball team, etc. – people/groups you participate in.*
>
> • **FOURTH Circle: The Circle of EXCHANGE**
> *List people you PAY to provide services in your life. (medical professionals, tax accountants, mechanics, hair dressers, barbers, teachers, etc.)*
>
> Note: People can be in more than one circle. Example: your doctor or teacher could also be a very close friend; a deceased parent/friend or even a pet, might be an intimate personal supporter, etc.

To illustrate, a high school teacher's experience using a circle of friends process will be described. This teacher decided to avoid burning out and wanted to inject life back into her students, herself, and the school. She knew she could not change everything, but she could make some changes for at least a few of her students who had been labeled "at risk", severely disabled and who were on the verge of dropping out of school. Her goal was to restore hope, and build relationships with other students.

Circle 1: The Circle of Intimacy

The teacher gathered about 50 students together and told them she wanted to have a frank discussion about friends and how to build more solid relationships in the school. She did not single out any individual, but talked in general for about half an hour about her own vision and beliefs in relationships and friendship as the core of a good school. She played music softly in the background and drew colorful images as she spoke. She then drew four concentric circles on the chalk board. She gave each student a sheet of paper that also had four concentric circles and requested that they put their name in the center of the inner circle. She modeled this by putting her name in the center of her circle. Then she directed them to write, on the first and smallest circle, the names of all the people closest to their heart and those that would make them miserable if they were no longer in their lives. She gave an example of her own life by putting her husband, her mother, her two children, and for fun her computer as she was an avid computer fan. She also put in the spirit of a friend of hers who had died two years prior.

Circle 2: The Circle of Friendship

Then she explained that the second circle was for people who were friends but not as close as those identified in the first circle. Again, she modeled this by using examples from her own life, she had six friends that she called all the time and two others who she saw once year but who called frequently. She also included some family members, a few teachers that she worked with, and her cat. She then asked the students to fill in their second circle, and found that the classroom was very quiet and that the students were taking this activity very seriously.

**Circle 3:
The Circle
of Participation**

The teacher explained that the third circle was for individuals or groups of people who they really liked but who were not very close. She modeled by identifying teachers at the high school, members of the church choir where she sings, her tennis partners, and members of her exercise class. She also listed individuals she sees occasionally, but who come and go, and three relatives she likes but seldom sees.

**Circle 4:
The Circle
of Exchange**

After the students had completed their third circle, she explained that the fourth circle was for people who are paid to be in their lives, such as teachers and doctors. She identified her doctor, chiropractor, and housekeeper as those people who were paid to be in her life. The students followed by identifying those people in their lives who were paid to be there. The circles were now complete.

The teacher told the students that she could tell a lot about a person by looking at their completed circles. She asked for a student to volunteer to share their completed circles. She held up the completed circles of the student who volunteered and read the names of the people in each circle. See Figure 2 for actual completed set of circles of a student who has a high quality of life experiences and opportunities. She stated that she had a full life, but not perfect. Then she showed the students, Jane, a completed set of circles that reflected a student who had disability and "at risk" labels and asked them to describe how they would feel if those were their circles. See Figure 3 for a completed set of circles reflecting students with disabilities and "at risk" labels. The most frequent response was that "the only people who are involved in this student's life were her family and those people who were paid to be there".

In addition the students also responded with the following descriptors:

How would you feel if you had no friends?

lonely	*depressed*
confused	*unwanted*
upset	*isolated*
rejected	*horrible*
isolated	*humorless*
distraught	*frustrated*
suicidal	

Then she asked the students to identify what they would do if this were representative of their life, and their responses were:

What would you do if you had no friends?

commit suicide   *kick*
die   *have a baby*
try to make friends   *take drugs*
move to a deserted island *drink*
do something really drastic *kill someone*
stay in bed
get a tutor

A passionate discussion poured out of the students. They began talking about all the pressures they feel from their families, the school, their teachers, and society in general. They identified that they felt "pressure" as they put it, "to look good, to do well and to achieve a lot." They felt the general attitude of teachers was that if they could not make it to university they were a total failure. The teacher listened and contributed to the discussion. She explained that she started the discussion to see how many students would be interested in helping her figure our how to fill in the circles of those students who were isolated and without friends.

For Friends and Intimacy: Build from the Outside In

She explained that her strategy would be to fill in circles from the outside circle inward. For example, if Jane were lonely, we would start by getting Jane involved in groups and organizations in order to gradually find people who would be more interested in more personal commitments. She explained that she was not asking "Who wants to be Jane's friend?" which is a question searching for failure. Rather, she would ask "Who knows Jane and is willing to brainstorm with me ideas for getting Jane more involved?". For example, if Jane likes films, maybe we could identify someone who could invite her to the film club.

The teacher asked the students if there was anyone who wanted to carry on this discussion and help to figure out ways to build community and circles in their school. To her surprise, all but three students signed up and said they wanted to meet again and often.

Circle of Friends is not a trick or a gimmick, it is a powerful tool. Like a chisel, it can be used to pry open ones heart, soul, and thoughts; or to create a work of art. A work of art does not happen overnight; neither does building circles or communities. Circles and community building is a commitment. It is as important as math, physics, or history. It is part of a curriculum of caring. It is holistic, powerful and not a thing you do once, then walk away. It is an ongoing strategy for growth, change, and development. A young man named Tracy, learned to read and write at the age of 33, after years believing he was "learning disabled" and a "retard". As an adult he spent time at a high school that was implementing circles and including all students in general education. He wondered what would have happened if someone would have gently and slowly helped him to build circles of friends and understand the difference between a drug pusher and a friend, a "gang" and a group of friends.

After hearing about and observing "circles" in action, he wrote the following powerful poem describing how circles are helping teachers and students not to pass each other without stopping, listening, and really seeing. This poem reflects the needs to be connected.

Don't Pass Me By

by Tracy LeQuyere

I'm a man at thirty-three
Who just learned to read,

I was here all the time
But people passed me by

One day a woman said
        I will show you a lie.
I know you can read with
        a little time.

But people just passed me by

So I gave me a little time,
And I gave her a little time.

See this writing,
I will have more time.

Don't pass me by.

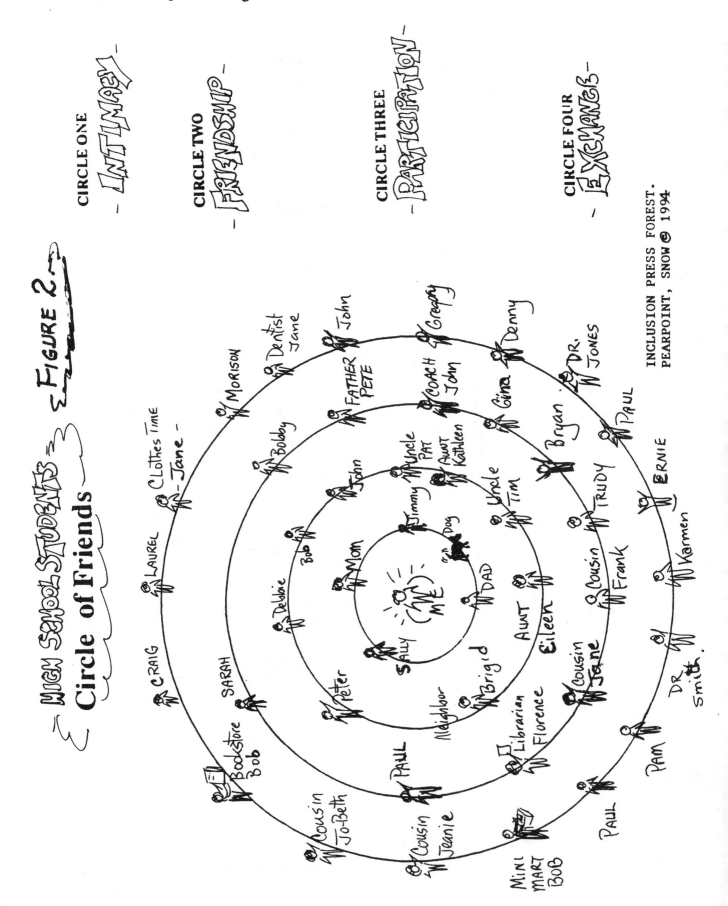

HIGH SCHOOL STUDENTS — FIGURE 2

Circle of Friends

CIRCLE ONE — INTIMACY —

CIRCLE TWO — FRIENDSHIP —

CIRCLE THREE — PARTICIPATION —

CIRCLE FOUR — EXCHANGE —

INCLUSION PRESS FOREST. PEARPOINT, SNOW © 1994

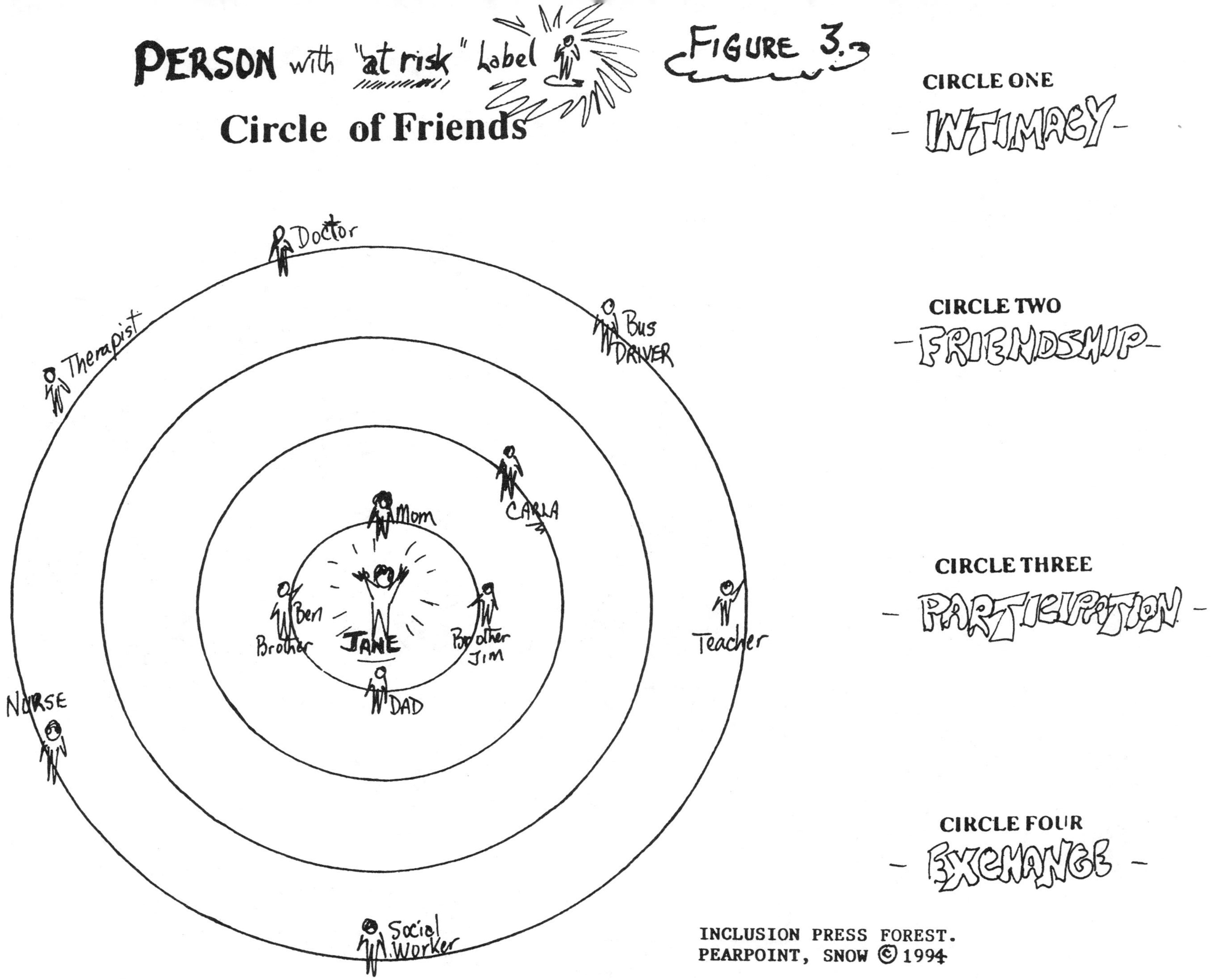

Figure 3.3

PERSON with "at risk" label
Circle of Friends

CIRCLE ONE
INTIMACY

CIRCLE TWO
FRIENDSHIP

CIRCLE THREE
PARTICIPATION

CIRCLE FOUR
EXCHANGE

INCLUSION PRESS FOREST.
PEARPOINT, SNOW © 1994

Mom
Brother Jim
Ben Brother
JANE
DAD

CARLA
Bus Driver
Teacher

Doctor
Therapist
Nurse
Social Worker

MAKING ACTION PLANS (MAPS)

MAPs are tools designed to help individuals, organizations, and families figure out how to move into the future effectively and creatively. MAPs is a tool that can be used by "artists" - artists dedicated to making people's lives better, richer, and stronger in the spiritual sense of life (Forest & Lusthaus, 1989; Forest & Lusthaus, 1990; Forest & Pearpoint, 1990; Vandercook, York, & Forest, 1989).

The MAPs process facilitates the collection of information about the persons and/or family in question. In his book entitled **Reflections on Inclusive Education** Patrick Mackan (1991) writes:

> *There is a temptation for teachers and other professionals to judge people in terms of their BEHAVIOR and outward appearance. It is all too seldom that we see through the apparent and visible which makes the person who has been wounded by rejection and segregation. We fail to realize that much behavior and acting out is not inherent but learned as a response to not being truly loved and accepted as a person. Masks are worn only as long as they are needed. Only genuine acceptance and a sense of belonging will lure the rejected supposedly inferior person out from behind the mask. (p.65)*

MAPs are tools held in the hand of a creative facilitator who can truly listen and hear the dream and the cry of pain of people or groups who have been rejected either overtly or covertly. The tool focuses on the positive, the gifts, and the strengths. The facilitator must first and foremost have a deep belief in the capacity of all human beings. The team facilitator must see the glass half full - not half empty. In this process we focus on the possibility of inclusive and heterogeneous communities that are based on the simple and yet profound premise that each person belongs, each can learn, and that in living we can discover the truth and dignity of each person.

There are eight key questions to MAPs as shown in Figure 4 (Forest & Pearpoint, 1992). Questions must all be asked but the order may be flexible based on the flow of the group dynamics and contributions. The following story is about a high school student named Donna who decided to have a MAPs process developed about her life and the future possibilities. Donna and her parents made up a "guest list" of whom they wanted to invite to the MAP session. Donna wrote a short note inviting each participant to her house on the day it was planned for:

Donna's Letter of Invitation to the MAPs participants

Dear Maya and David,

I want to invite you to my meeting to help me think about my future. It's going to be on Saturday, Nov. 14 at 10 am at my house. We are going to have lunch when it is done. I hope you can come.

Donna

Donna's Parents Letter of Invitation to the MAPs participants

Dear Friends,

As you know Donna is just starting a process call MAPS. The purpose of this tool is to help her and us make that awesome transition from being a kid to being an adult who is a full-fledged member of the community.

The first meeting will be Nov. 14 and Donna chose you as guests of honor. We all put a list together of everybody Donna knows, including her peers and some adults. She went through the list and circled the names of those she wanted around her, helping her to start to think about her future. Yours are the names she circled. This means you are the people she trusts the most and with whom she feels most comfortable. You are the ones with whom she is willing to put herself in a vulnerable position to discuss her real wants an concerns. You are her circle of support, the people she can really talk to (and you all know how tough that can be). Many of you are part of our circle of support too, but this is Donna's list, 100%.

So please join us on Sat., Nov. 14 at our home. We'll start at 10 AM and have lunch (yes, Taco salad!). Marsha Forest and Jack Pearpoint will be the facilitators. I think this will be an interesting morning.

Love
Mark and Christina

Other MAPs have been held in classrooms, school cafeterias, corporate board rooms, small offices, and so forth. The key for an individual or group is to voluntarily choose to explore with the process, and for those people to choose whom else they want to invite. It is not a case conference or IEP where the person is the guest and professionals are in control. Here the key people are the "person" herself and those he or she invites. The person will define her own problems, dreams, nightmares, and so forth with a little help from her friends.

Donna's parents also wrote a note and sent it to the people who Donna had decided to invite to her MAPs process.

Fifteen people were invited and 16 people came. The church minister heard about the gathering and invited himself. Donna, of course agreed. It is interesting to note that people are truly honored to be asked to attend a serious session about a person's life. In this case, two people came significant distances to participate. They cared. People really do care and want to be involved.

It is often better to have a facilitator or two who are immersed in the process and who do not know the assembled cast of characters. The facilitators can then bring out the information without a preconceived scenario. People are invited to be involved in a process that is time limited, that is in Donna's case, she invited people for the morning followed by an optional lunch.

Where to begin.

Everyone is seated comfortably facing a wall with large sheets of paper. A process facilitator acts as the "host". This person welcomes the group, explains the process, guides the questions and keeps the session paced and on track. A second facilitator is the "graphic guide". He or she records, listens, and creates a colorful record of the proceedings. In addition, the session could be audio recorded for those who access information better auditoraly then visually. The public record is an essential part of the MAPs process. A personal, comfortable and informal atmosphere is essential. The facilitator urges everyone to trust and be honest with one another, and not to use jargon or initials that would be mystery to the others present. The process facilitator begins by asking everyone to introduce themselves and share their relationship to the key person.

For example:

"Hi, I'm Wayne; I've known Donna since she was born."

"I've been friends of Mark and Christina's for over 20 years."

"Donna was in my choir class during junior high school."

"Hi, I am Donna's boyfriend, Sam, and I am going to marry her."

Question #1:
What's a MAP?

The facilitator should welcome the group, make them feel comfortable, then review the purpose, the specific questions to be asked, and a give general description of what will happen. When people are ready, the participants are asked, *"What is a MAP?"* Some of the answers from Donna's team were:

- helps you get from one place an another;
- a guide;
- a way to go from here to there.

The process facilitator then said, *"that's exactly what we are here for, we want to help Donna get from where she's at today to where she's going. We want this day to be a guide of how to go from here to there."* A perfect start.

If you don't know where you're going, then any way will do.
        Lewis Carroll

Question #2:
What is person's history or story?

In order to get the entire cast of characters into the act, telling the family or individual's story is requested. A time limit is set, as stories can go on forever, what is important are the essentials as the family or school sees it. Donna's story has been heard before about other children with disability labels; it started with, fear, disappointment, and rejection. Then through tremendous effort on the part of her family they changed the initial expectations and realities in the community, and across the family to some levels of acceptance in regular school, regular classes and church. This story has difficult twists and turns and very emotional parts with intense medical stories. Donna has Down Syndrome, visual impairment, and diabetes. The graphics facilitator drew the story and then summarized. At the end of each question the facilitator checks to be sure the emerging picture represents what was really said and if there is anything to add. This check constantly reaffirms the ownership of the MAP to the participants. The facilitators are pulling out information, drawing a map so that they can start on a process to reach the dream.

Question #3:
What are your dreams?

This question is very important so the person and the participants know where to go in developing the eventual plan of action. Donna was abundantly clear. *"My dream is to marry Sam and to be a star! I want babies. I want to live here and have friends like Greg. I also want to perform on stage with Paul Simon"*. The facilitator asked Donna to expand on her dream and she also asked everyone else to simply listen and not add anything. She said: *"This is your dream Donna — go for it. What do you really want to see in your future. Tell the graphic facilitator to draw exactly what you want."* Donna was crystal clear about this dream. Figure 5 is the graphic display of Donna's dream.

The dream question is the heart and soul of the MAPs process. The facilitator must get out the real dream and be totally non-judgmental. Facilitators must be sure their body language does not negatively effect the process. Once a facilitator totally shut down the entire process at this point for Jason, who was described by his school teacher as a major behaviour problem, BD, and BAD. He (Jason) hardly spoke until his first MAPs. He declared in the dream question that he wanted to be a doctor. The facilitator, who knew him, literally stopped the process and said: *"That's ridiculous!"*, ... *" You can't even do your homework."* The MAPs process ended immediately. At the next MAP, with a new facilitator, Jason again spoke about his dream. This time it was drawn and listened to with a full and accepting heart by the facilitator. As the MAP unfolded, Jason himself modified his dream. **We have learned that in the seed of all dreams is the essence of a person's real desire and what might eventually be feasible.** Jason really did not want to be a doctor; however, he wanted respect, and he wanted to work around hospitals where his dad had worked. He liked the people at the hospital and he had been helped by a wonderful doctor friend.

You see things and say "Why?" But I dream things that never were and say "Why not?"

G.B. Shaw

The MAPS Mandala

Introductions:
Who is present?
What is their
relationship to
the person?

What is the
Story?
History?

What is the
Dream?

What is a
MAP?

What is the
Nightmare?

What is the
Plan of Action
to avoid the
Nightmare and to
make the Dream
come true?

Who is the
Person?
brain storm

What are the
Person's Needs?
What do **We**
need to do to
Meet these Needs?

What is the
Person
Good at...
strengths,
gifts,
talents?

JACK PEARPOINT

© Inclusion Press 1992

Judith Snow, one of Canada's leading experts on the rights of people who have been excluded, wanted in her dream to be a truck driver. Judith uses a wheel chair and has no mobility except for the use of her right thumb. *"A truck driver!"* many exclaimed. But Judith has taught many of us that to be a truck driver means motion, movement, freedom, travel, adventure, and seeing the world from high up. She is living the essence of her dream today, even though there is not a truck in her life - yet. We need to see people's dreams not as concrete or etched in stone, but as beautiful fluid messages and images of what is possible. Many at Donna's MAP were terrified of Donna being married and having children. *"After all she was a person with Down Syndrome. She could not care for children, she should not..."* People were asked to listen respectfully and NOT make judgments.

The Dream Catcher

As the legend goes, the Dream Catcher was used by the Woodland Indians and was hung in the lodge. It's use was to catch all dreams, good or bad. The bad dreams (nightmares) would get caught up in the webbing and be held there till first morning light, then burned off. Now, the good dreams were caught, and knowing their way to the hole in the center, would filter down into the feathers and be held there, only to return another night, to be dreamed again.

Question #4:
What are your nightmares?

Without a vision, the people perish.
Proverbs

As a facilitator, the scariest question is the nightmare. We do not want people to feel bad or sad. But the nightmare and the dream are equal in importance. It is the nightmare that we want to avoid - yet most of our "programs" and "projects" often fuel the nightmare rather than the dream. For example, many parents of children with disabilities answer the nightmare question with this response: *"I fear my son/daughter will end up in an institution"*. The traditional special education service delivery model that segregates students with disabilities from their non-disabled neighbours and peers essentially is preparing those students for a segregated adult life style such as that found in institutions. We have never heard a nightmare that had to do with getting bad grades, getting a less then a perfect job. It is always about more fundamental stuff - loneliness, poverty, and death. The dream empowers families, people, organizations to dream again. The nightmare allows people the dignity to let their monsters and demons out of the closet in an atmosphere where it is heard, recorded, respected, planned for avoiding, and then we move on. The entire aim of the MAP process is to actualize the dream and avoid the nightmare. Can there be a guarantee? Absolutely not! Does the process at least allow the chance of survival? Absolutely! The process promises nothing, however, it gives hope. The opposite of hope is despair and there is far too much of that going around these days - especially in schools.

Question #5:
Who is the person?

This is a brainstorming step. Everyone is asked to throw words into the air and the facilitator records them as a portrait of the person. Not just good words or bad words - just words that pop into the participants heads as to who the person really is. This time the person is asked to listen. In Donna's situation a large outline of a person was drawn and the facilitator gave each participant two "post-its" to write their thoughts on. The graphic facilitator grouped words in themes. The person, Donna, is asked to identify their own words to describe themselves, and then to choose three favourite words from all the descriptions. Donna chose: *"In love, loving, and risk taker".*

To demonstrate the power of the words identified to this question , sometimes the facilitator asks: what others not present have called the person in the past? In Jason's case, for example, the words others used were "trouble-maker", bad, behaviour disordered, and manic-depressive. None of those showed up at the MAP. Instead there were words like: energetic, active, stubborn, tense, intense, terrific, energy, and so forth.

Thomas Armstrong (1989, p. 128) illustrated this with his suggestions of how to "turn lead into gold":

Turning Lead into Gold

Thomas Armstrong

A child who is judged to be:	*Can also be considered:*
learning disabled	learning different
hyperactive	a kinesthetic learner
dyslexic	a spatial learner
aggressive	assertive
plodding	thorough
lazy	relaxed
immature	late blooming
phobic	cautious
scattered	divergent
daydreaming	imaginative
irritable	sensitive
preservative	persistent

Question #6:
What are the person's strengths, gifts, and talents?

Here the concept of "giftedness" is stressed, not as an academic ability, but as a totally rounded person. The graphic facilitator can draw for this image a gift box with gifts coming out of an opening box. As the participants identify descriptions that identify the person's gifts, strengths, and talents they are written down and stated very positively. Some of Donna's gifts identified by the participants were:

> *her smile*
> *personality*
> *family*
> *spirit*
> *lovingness...*

Budgets have deficits.
People have Gifts!
> *Forest/Pearpoint*

Question #7:
What does the person need?

The complete question is: **What does the person need to achieve the dream and avoid the nightmare?** The dream and nightmare are the anchor points of the MAPs process. Once we understand them, we have a foundation on which to make daily decisions. Put simply, we say "yes" to things that will lead in the direction of the dream, and "no" to choices that promote the nightmare.

In answering this question, the participants must think about what it will take, people and resources to make the dream come true. There was complete agreement that Donna needed friends her own age to be more included with other typical high school students at church and at school. It was also agreed that her parents needed some time alone to get their own lives in order. This information can really help to focus the opportunities that need to be created for the person and the formal and informal supports needed.

Question #8
What is the plan of action?

In order to prevent the nightmares from happening and to facilitate the dreams becoming true, the participants are asked to, in a very specific way, identify the plans. These plans should include "who will do what, and when will they do it". Donna's plan involved several important components:

- Increase the circle of friends at high school.

- Increase the circle of friends at church.

- Train friends and others to be able to deal with Donna's insulin reading and monitoring.

- Maintain the regular high school class participation.

- Investigate possible "Self Advocacy" support groups.

- Investigate stage performing possibilities at school, church, and in the community.

- Investigate the possibility of working as an assistant in the child-care program located on the High School campus.

- Identify opportunities for Donna to present at local, state and national conferences advocating for individuals, related to her dream to perform on stage.

This process took about 90 minutes and no one was tired or bored. The process has been completed with students who no one believed would sit still for 5 minutes, and they do. For very young children, we have invited them to be present for as long as they wish and have people available for child care when they decide to leave.

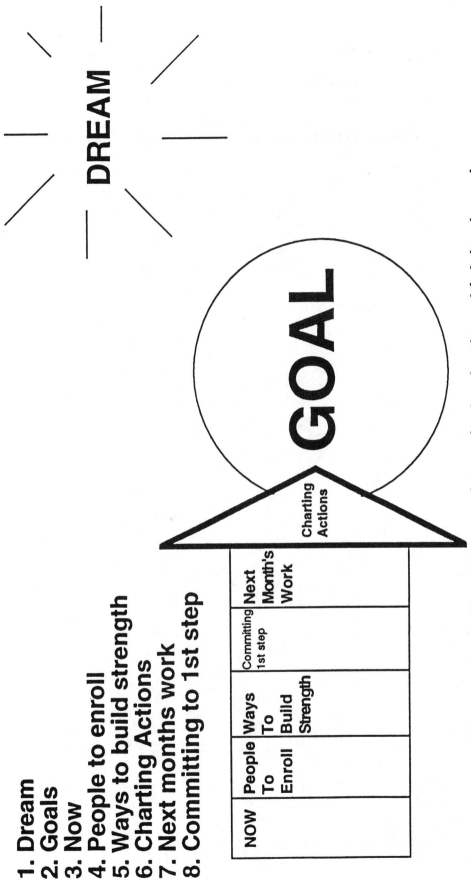

DREAM

GOAL

1. Dream
2. Goals
3. Now
4. People to enroll
5. Ways to build strength
6. Charting Actions
7. Next months work
8. Committing to 1st step

NOW	People To Enroll	Ways To Build Strength	Committing 1st step	Next Month's Work
				Charting Actions

Situate yourself in a very positive future - picture it clearly, then think backwards

1. Touching the Dream
2. Sensing the Goal: Focus for the next year
3. Grouping in the Now: Where am I/are we?
4. Identifying people to enroll on the journey
5. Recognizing Ways to Build strength
6. Charting actions for the next few months
7. Planning the next months work
8. Committing to the next step

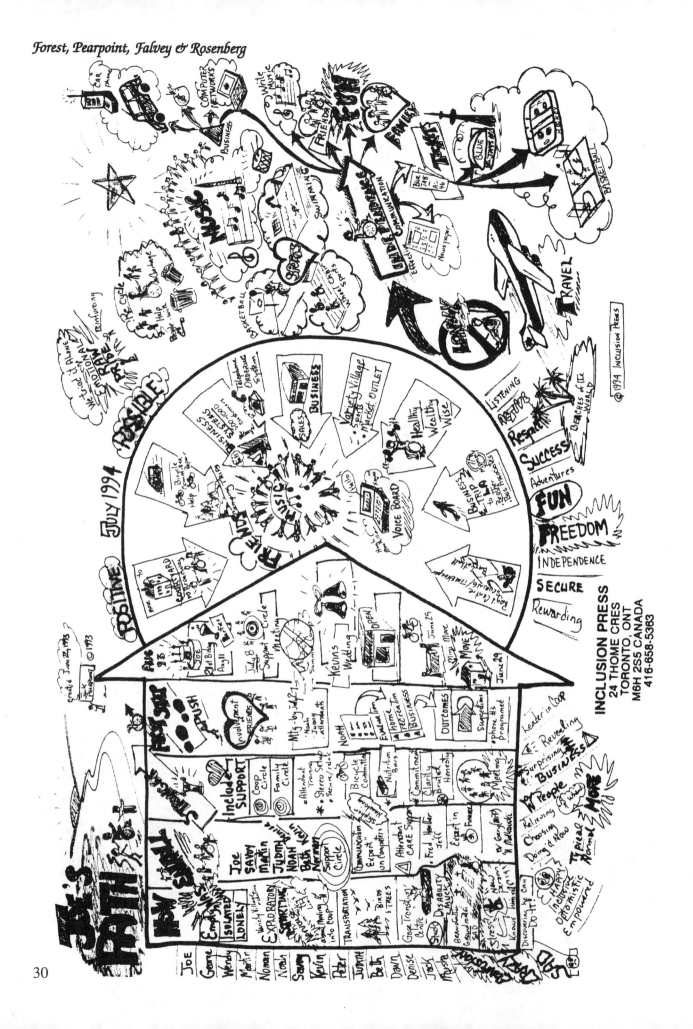

PATH

PLANNING ALTERNATIVE TOMORROWS WITH HOPE

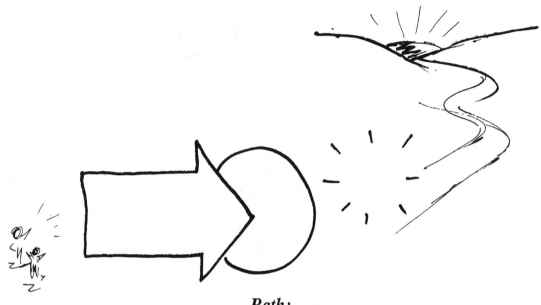

Path:

route, itinerary, course,
track, run, line, road,
circuit, tour, orbit, walk.

Roget's Thesaurus

PATH evolved from the MAPS process. It was designed and developed by Jack Pearpoint, John O'Brien and Marsha Forest beginning in 1991. It offers an opportunity to extend the MAPs steps and to put into place a plan of action. PATH may be a self sustaining planning process. See Figure 6 for the outline of the PATH and Figure 7 for a sample PATH graphically represented. PATH, as in the Circle and MAPS, is another tool to address long and short range planning. This is another eight step process – it is an exercise in thinking backwards. Once again, this process is best undertaken with a process facilitator and a graphic recorder who graphically presents the information expressed.

Schools that are involved in long range planning for students, the student body, the school, and the community, have experienced new roles and functions. In this new role, students, teachers, parents, community members, and friends are invited to participate. The teacher's task is to identify the strengths of each student and to nurture that strength as a catalyst to explore the full range of every student's capacities. By inviting the full participation of the others in "figuring it out", no teacher is given the impossible charge of "knowing it all", or being responsible to teach everyone. Everyone becomes a member of the team with the problems and challenges becoming shared goals, the spectrum of talents and energy available are quite impressive.

In order to provide an example of the PATH process Barry, a seventh grader, who uses a wheelchair, and has a communicator will be shared. He lives at home with a number of brothers, sisters, aunts, uncles, and his mother. He has shared with his teacher that he is not happy at home. His means of communication is using a head pointer and a typewriter, some verbal communication and head nodding. At this time Barry chose not to have his mother or sister at the meeting. The meeting included Barry, his teacher, the teaching assistant, three of his friends from school, the student teacher, and his caseworker. These are all people who he trusts and feels comfortable discussing very private things.

Step 1 - The North Star - the Dream

The time is spent focusing on the individual identifying his or her DREAMS and ultimately their North Star. Some of the questions that can assist a person identify their North Star may be:

- What ideals do you most want to realize?
- What values do you want to guide you?
- What gives direction to your life?
- What drives you?

Barry's North Star was: to be able to live in a home with just a few people, he wanted support so that he could eat when he wanted to, go to the bathroom when he wanted to, have a bath when he wanted one, and leave the house when he wanted to. The facilitator finished this step by summarizing the dream and solicited from Barry his perspective on the accuracy of the information that had been graphically depicted.

Step 2 - The Goal

The second step is to choose a future time just beyond where we can predict comfortably - say 6 months, a year, two years- and go there for a few minutes. It is very important to assist the group in this visualization/planning activity. The facilitator may suggest that everyone get in a time capsule. In that time capsule it is now in the future and everyone is going to share what has happened. The facilitator coaches everyone to remember events from a **POSITIVE** and **POSSIBLE** future. The qualification is important. Some good things may not be possible in the time frame.

Coach people to remember positive events that have occurred (remember they really haven't occurred). The facilitator says *"I remember a couple of months ago was Barry's birthday, and he received a Game Boy for his birthday"*...

Ask the person and the group to share what has occurred. This is the development of the GOALS for the person. The facilitator will try to have the individual describe what it felt like, what the smells were, tastes, touches, and overall feelings in the past.

Barry put in his goal 1 year down the road that he would be going to High School and would have more friends. Barry stated he went on a number of field trips. In the past he had not been able to go because his mother did not send the permission slip. He stated that he received a new light weight electric wheelchair and a new communicator that was easier to use and be understood by others. His friends added that their parents brought Barry to birthday parties with them on weekends. He went to the Computer Access Center and they completed a consultation and recommended the school look into Macintosh computers with adaptations for Barry. The most important goal was that Barry had been able to talk with his mother and really communicate with her.

Step 3 - Now

The third step is to bring everyone back to the **Present** - reality. The facilitator asks the participant: "What is it like now? Not good words or bad words - just a snap-shot of what life looks like now."

Barry and the group generated words like: lonely, stressful, scared of his mother, hard, tiring, scary, fun and safe at school, exciting, have lots of friends. The PATH process now, is a visual representation of the differences between NOW on the left - with the positive possible future (goal) - and the North Star Dream on the right. The facilitator helps the participants to see that this difference is often necessary and good to move forward. In PATH, the facilitator now takes more control by simply declaring that for the purposes of the PATH, the objective will be to get from NOW to the GOAL (in the time span articulated). The facilitator finishes this step by summarizing the individual's sense of the now and getting confirmation that the summary is accurate.

Step 4 - Who Do We Enroll?

To accomplish this , the facilitator points out that there are some preconditions. First, no one can do this alone, thus the fourth question is, *"Who do you need to enroll to achieve you Goal?"* Again, this supports the notion that we are striving for everyone to be interdependent, not independent, we all work as teams and we all depend on each other.

It is entirely acceptable that people may say "funders", "government", "_____agency", and so forth or a whole range of generic groups that need to be enrolled. However, the facilitator needs look for specific persons or contact persons with each agency. Participants should be encouraged to enroll themselves to assist.

Barry said he was going to enroll his teacher and the teaching assistant to begin really communicating with his mother. Barry asked his friends to help him get to parties, if needed he would take his old flexible wheelchair.

This process of enrolling others means more than just getting permission to participate, it means one is sharing and making a commitment in the persons life. This step also recognizes those people with whom the individual wants to build a shared commitment. When the facilitator is confident the list is complete, he/she will remind everyone this is a process and one can add, change, and delete as long as the significant participant agrees, here as well as any other place along the PATH. At this time the facilitator will also review the PATH and add any names or resources needed. Then the facilitator will have the group share some feeling words associated with the list of people enrolled and what they are enrolled to do.

Step 5 - Getting Stronger

The fifth step is about getting stronger. The facilitator coaches the group through the reality that in order to enroll people and to move from now to the future, an enormous amount of work will be required. This will be added to every-one's already busy life. So the real question is to focus: *"What do we need to do as a group, team, and/or family, in order to be strong enough to reach the goal and keep this team moving forward. Similarly, what does each person have to do to be strong enough to be able to make their contribution at the personal level."*

Barry's list contained:

- Having teachers and teaching assistants to share and communicate with.

- Communicate effectively with his mother.

- Being able to get out to purchase personal items.

- Time to cry if and when needed.

- Support me, for I fear rejection of my mother.

- Getting involved in social groups.

- Learning from adults with disabilities about what they are able to do and how.

Step 6 - 3 Months

In the process of events, the next two steps are similar. Again, the facilitator gives directions and takes the group into a much closer future - such as three months from today. Coaching everyone to think positively, assume that things have been going really well. The direction of the progress is correct, people are feeling some momentum. What has happened already. The easiest way to do this is to pick a clear element in the Goal; and think of what has happened already. If there is time, the facilitator can explore several of the elements to see what steps were (are to be) implemented within the three months.

The facilitator must be extremely time conscious at this time point, and it is good to point out to the participants that it is unlikely that every detail of the PATH will be completed at this time. However, once the process is understood, people can fill in their details later.

Wishing never
filled a game bag.
Maori Wisdom

Step 7- 1 Month

The seventh step is a repeat of the sixth – except that the time is even closer to today, one month. What is important at this step is to push everyone for very precise specific steps:

- Who will do what?
- When will they do it?
- Where?

Some members of the group find this very difficult as the people realize that this exercise is getting out of the dreaming process, and very close to reality. This step is also used to identify specifics for the more immediate future and can be used to measure peoples true commitment.

Step 8 - The First Step (s)

The Final step is the **FIRST STEP**. What is the first step? The facilitator should insist that this be some action that can be taken almost immediately - i.e. by tomorrow or next week. It does not need to be gigantic - but if the process is going to begin, it is essential that it begin **NOW**.

If someone has to make a phone call, a target should be set: *"by noon tomorrow..."*. If someone has to contact the funding agency, then: *"by tomorrow the agency will be called."*.

At this point as well as through the process, it is essential that the goal of interdependence be at the forefront. All the participants must form a new habit of asking for support and not assuming everything should be done. Many times the first step does not flow, that is OK, it is up to the group and the facilitator to see if there is a block. In many situations something or someone is standing in the way of progress. The PATH is a means to identify those blocks and then take the steps to deal with the blocks. The block could be funding, medical, social, emotional, and so forth. The energy and commitment of the team, at this time, must come together to strategize any and all blocks that are identified.

Closure is important in any process. The facilitator asks the group to simply give a word or a phrase about what they felt and about the process. Barry offered: excited and scared, others offered: trusting, energized, go for it. The excitement and reality of this process is in the implementation and the follow-up.

Each facilitator or co-facilitator will have their own unique style and character. The goal is that the meeting and the process remained focused on the individual, and that the individual and his or her significant others have a say in the development of the process. It is up to the team to allow that dream and North Star to become a reality.

CONSIDERATIONS/ CAUTIONS

There are several cautions and considerations that should be considered when using any of the three mentioned strategies, that is Circle of friends, MAPs, and/or PATH are presented below.

• The facilitator always needs to remember the process is for, by and with the individual; the facilitator needs to continually return to the individual and be sure what is going on the wall is accurate, relevant, meaningful, and true.

• Various communication means maybe necessary to assure the focus person is involved, understands, and a true participant. One may utilize facilitated communication, pictures, or someone else speaking and the individual verifying with a head nod or eye wink. The process has been successful with individuals who are very verbal as well as individuals who do not communicate using standard means.

• Trust and confidentiality are two issues that must be addressed and reinforced. The process places the focus person in a vulnerable position, and the facilitator must assure the person, and remind the participants, that this meeting is very personal and confidential.

• It is important that the facilitator and the participants discuss when the process will be implemented and when results may be observed. The focus person may become excited by the process and then become extremely frustrated when the dream or North Star does not come true within a week. Timing is sensitive and area issue that must be addressed within the process.

• The facilitator must be sure that a support process is in place for all participants to deal with the excitement, and any other emotions that may have been brought out as a result of the process.

• Remember this is not a trick/gimmick or quick fix. The three tools are all long range planning processes. The process will bring people together to have a common vision for a person, family, or organization. It will take time, commitment, and knowledge to follow through what has been generated by the Circle of Friends, MAP, and/or PATH (Forest & Pearpoint, 1992).

• Recognizing that the three processes outlined are very personal, it is sometimes, but not always, a good strategy to provide the questions to the person ahead of time to allow them to review the questions and feel comfortable with the process.

• The MAPs and PATH processes do not to replace the Individualized Educational Plan (IEP). They can be used to generate meaningful information for an IEP, and thus be very complementary, however MAPs and PATH are not the IEP.

• The process is similar to Transition Planning for the school to adult transition process. The outcome of a PATH can be presented as a Individualized Transition Plan.

• The process should not be controlled by experts and is not simply an academic exercise. The process is to be a means to develop Person Centered Planning leading to people working together for the common goals and dreams of an individual, family or organization. See Figure 8 for a customer driven service delivery system. Figure 8 represents the interpretation of an organization (CITY) and how the planing process can work for an individual.

PATH was recently used by Marsha and Jack in the Forest Grove School District (Forest Grove, Oregon) with 300 participants. The invitation came from Irv Nikolai, Superintendent of the District, and engaged students, parents, teachers, administration and board members in creating a shared vision of the future of their school.

SUMMARY

The value of friends and colleagues cannot be emphasized enough. In order to embrace all children within our schools, schools need to look different and how educators develop services in schools needs to look different. It is also important for school to reflect in their educational service delivery model the principle that all children belong and all children want to belong. This booklet has provided three ways to change how schools look and how services are developed.

And the song
from beginning
to end,
I found in
the heart of
a friend.
          Longfellow

*[For individuals or groups who want to use the PATH planning process, we **strongly urge** you to use the **PATH Workbook** and the **PATH Training video** available through **Inclusion Press**. Ordering information is at the end of this booklet.]*

Community-Focused Customer Driven

STEPS	ME	CITY
Getting Organized	Who can help? When can we get together? Invite the group. What's the process?	Establish a process. Find a place. Start the paperwork process.
Assessing My Needs	What do I want? What are my dreams? Where am I today?	Facilitate a futures planning meeting. Record the information.
Building my TEAM	Who else can help? What do I need to do?	Identify others who can assist. Keep the process in focus. Provide coordination.
Developing The Plan	How does it happen? How is it coordinated? Who does what?	Provide documentation. Establish serivce plans with Outcomes & Measures for review.
Taking the 1st Steps	What should I do first? Planning the next month's work. How do I know my plan is working?	Help set priorities. Secure funding/resources agreements. Begin collection of service data.

MISSION: Services That Make

Services Planning and Delivery System

STEPS	ME	CITY
Things go wrong sometimes!	This is unexpected! How do I fix it? I need help - Who shall I ask?	Be available and responsive. Handle emergency issues.
Making minor corrections.	This is scary! I need some support!	Be flexible. Be alert to small things before they get big.
Comprehensive Service Plan Review based on my outcomes.	Let's see how things are going. This is working fine! This needs attention!	Establish regular review process. Gather data.
This stuff works!	This is working fine, lets keep on. This needs some attention, lets make some changes.	Facilitate documentation reporting and service plan adjustment approvals.
Why isn't everthing this easy?	I'm delighted! I hope everyone else has it this good! Now, I think I would like to..............	Fade to the background. Develop strengths and skills. Be available.

A Difference - 1 ☻ @A ⏻

Recommended Viewing and Reading:

Videos:

PATH Training Video (1994) - 35 minutes

PATH Demonstration Video (1993) - 58 minutes

With a Little Help From My Friends (1990) - 58 minutes

Kids Belong Together (1990) - 30 minutes

Miller's Map (1992) - 30 minutes

Dreamcatchers (1993) - 15 minutes

Friends of ... Clubs (1993) - 15 minutes

Books:

PATH, a workbook for planning positive possible futures. Pearpoint, J., O'Brien, J. & Forest, M. (1993) Toronto: Inclusion Press.

Action for Inclusion. O'Brien, J. & Forest, M. with Snow, Pearpoint & Hasbury (1989) Toronto: Inclusion Press.

The Inclusion Papers, Strategies to Make Inclusion Work. Pearpoint, J., Forest, M., & Snow, J. (1992) Toronto: Inclusion Press.

From Behind the Piano: the building of Judtih Snow's unique circle of friends. Pearpoint, J. (1990) Toronto: Inclusion Press.

Don't Pass Me By. Bunch, G.W. (1991). Toronto: Inclusion Press.

Reflections on Inclusive Education. Mackan, P. (1991) Toronto: Inclusion Press.

All these titles are available from :

Inclusion Press

24 Thome Cres.
Toronto, ONT.
Canada M6H 2S5

    Phone: 416-658-5363
    Fax: 416-658-5067

Circle of Support (Friends)

First Circle: *Circle of INTIMACY*

Second Circle: *Circle of FRIENDSHIP*

Third Circle: *Circle of PARTICIPATION*

Fourth Circle: *Circle of EXCHANGE*

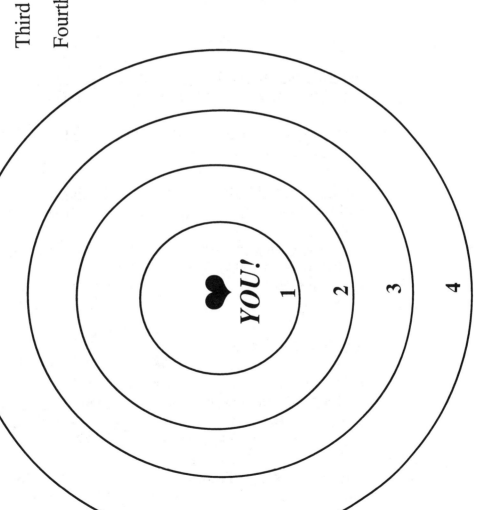

Fill Circles from the Outside–In!

References

Asher, S.R., Odem, S.L., & Gottman, J.M. (1977). Children's friendships in school settings. In L.G. Katz (Ed.), **Current topics in early childhood education** (Vol. 1, pp. 33-61). Norwood, NJ.: Ablex.

Bunch, G.W. (1991) **Don't Pass Me By: writings from the street.** , Toronto, Inclusion Press

Condeluci, Al. (1991) **Interdependence the route to community**. Orlando, FL.: Paul M. Deutsch Press, Inc.

Forest, M. & Lusthaus, E. (1990) Everyone belongs with the MAPs action planning system. **Teaching Exceptional Children. 22** (2), 32-35.

Forest, M. & Lusthaus, E. (1989). Promoting educational equality for all students: Circles and MAPs. In Stainback, S., Stainback, W., & Forest, M. (Eds.). **Educating all students in the mainstream of regular education** (pp.43-58). Baltimore, MD.: Paul H. Brookes Publishing Co.

Forest, M. & Pearpoint, J. (1992) Everyone belongs: building the vision with MAPs - the McGill Action Planning System. In D. Wetherow (Ed.). **The whole community catalogue: Welcoming people with disabilities into the heart of community life** (pp. 95-99) Manchester, CT.: Communitas, Inc.

Forest, M. & Pearpoint, J. (1992) Putting all kids on the MAP. **Educational Leadership** Vol. 50, #2 Oct. 1992

Ginott, H. (1972) **Teacher and Child**

Grenot-Scheyer, M., Coots, J., & Falvey, M.A. (1989) Developing and fostering friendships. In M. Falvey **Community-based curriculum: Instructional strategies for students with severe disabilities** (pp. 345-358). Baltimore, MD.: Paul H. Brookes Publishing Co.

Hartup, W.W. (1975). The origins of friendship. In M. Lewis & L.A. Rosenblum (Eds.), **Friendships and peer relations** (pp. 11-26). New York: John Wiley & Sons.

Howes, C. (1983). Patterns of friendship. **Child Development, 54**, 1041-1053.

LeQuyere, Tracy (1991). **Don't Pass Me By.** edited: G.Bunch. Toronto: Inclusion Press.

Lewis, M., & Rosenblaum, L.A. (Eds.) (1975). **Friendships and peer relations**. New York: John Wiley & Sons.

Mackan, P. (1991) **Reflections on Inclusive Education.** Toronto: Inclusion Press.

O'Brien, J. & Forest, M. with Snow, Pearpoint & Hasbury (1989) **Action for Inclusion.** Toronto: Inclusion Press.

Pearpoint, J., Forest, M., & Snow, J. (1992) **The Inclusion Papers, Strategies to Make Inclusion Work.** Toronto: Inclusion Press.

Pearpoint, J., O'Brien, J. & Forest, M. (1993) **PATH, a workbook for planning positive possible futures.** Toronto: Inclusion Press.

Pearpoint, J. (1990) **From Behind the Piano: the building of Judtih Snow's unique circle of friends.** Toronto: Inclusion Press.

Perske, R. (1989). **Circles of friends**. Nashville, TN: Abingdon Press.

Sherwood, S.K. (1990) A circle of friends in a 1st grade classroom. **Educational Leadership, 48** (3), 41.

Stainback, W. & Stainback, S. (1990). Facilitating peer supports and friendships. In W. Stainback & S. Stainback (Eds.). **Support networks for inclusive integrated education** (pp51-64). Baltimore, MD: Paul H. Brookes Publishing Co.

Stainback, W., Stainback, S., & Wilkinson, A. (1992) Encouraging peer supports and friendships. **Teaching Exceptional Children. 24** (2), 6-11.

Strully, J. & Strully, C. (1985). Friendship and our children. **Journal for The Association for Persons with Severe Handicaps**, 10 (4), 224-227.

SHAFIK'S MAP
THE NEW MAPS TRAINING VIDEO
- a Transcript -

PART 1: SHAFIK'S MAP

NARRATION

Marsha: Hello I'm Marsha Forest

Jack: And I'm Jack Pearpoint we're here to examine the MAPS process. We're going to use segments from a MAP we shot with Shafik, a Community organizer and Human rights activist in Philadelphia. We're going to use segments from this MAP to demonstrate the principles and practices of the MAPS Process.

Marsha: What you're going to see is John O'Brien as the process facilitator of the MAPS process. John along with Judith Snow, Jack Pearpoint and myself are the developers of the MAPS process. David Hasbury is the graphic recorder in this video.

GETTING STARTED

Jack: As we are starting a MAP, the **location** is very important. We want it to be laid back relaxed and comfortable for people. Sitting around a board table isn't a great idea. It's important that there will be a graphic and people face it. We want everyone to be able to see the color and images as they emerge and interact with it. We want the participants to see each other face to face so creating a comfortable location where people can talk to each other is essential to an effective MAP.

Marsha: The first question everyone asks is **who should attend** a MAP. The answer is it could be two or twenty-two people, but the best participants are those who know the person or the organization best. In this case, Shafik invited Shina, who is his wife, Bahiya, who is his very best friend and most important colleague, and much to our honour he invited Jack and I to participate in this his MAP.

TRANSCRIPT of the MAP

John O'Brien: Shafik, is there a way for you to start a meeting like this, a way to get people centered on what's going on and to get people started?

Shafik: One of the things I think is important for people to do, by way of knowing who is around them is to visualize a symbol that is their symbol and explain themselves in relationship to that symbol. My symbol is my marriage ring, my marriage piece. It is a symbol of an Ankh which represents eternal life. Personally right now I'm in a struggle for life. I think its appropriate that I start off by offering this symbol to my collective and introduce myself in relationship to my whole being to stay alive, and to stay healthy because I have a lot of work to do. (note: Shafik is struggling with bone cancer and is in constant treatment for this.)

Shina: In terms of symbols I think for me right now this one that I wear around my neck is most important to me. It has a turquoise stone which is a healing stone and I also am dealing with cancer in my own life. It's special to me that I wear it as it gives be both power and strength.

Marsha: When I came out of my breast cancer surgery five years ago, Jack put this around my neck. It is the only piece of jewellery I wear and for me it represents a healing circle.

Bahiya: The symbol I'd like to offer is a symbol of my chains because these represent my connectedness to Shafik. Much of who I am and where I am in my life today is because we have met and are partners in travelling this journey together.

Jack: My symbol is a Maori pendant given to me by Te Ripowai Higgins in New Zealand. Its translation is "binder of people".

NARRATION

Jack: The MAPS process is exploratory. It gathers information and organizes it around a person or an organization. In this case, a good facilitator has to get people relaxed, has to demystify the process and get people ready for the MAP. In Shafik's case we are charting unmapped, unknown territory so it's a very exciting adventure.

TRANSCRIPT continued:

John O'Brien: We have a simple process to work through and we call it a MAP. I think there are two kinds of MAPS, one kind of MAP is where you're trying to figure out how to get from here to somewhere that's already located on a MAP. Most of the ones we do we know where we're going. We know that we're going to end up with somebody in school where they belong or we know we're going to end up with somebody in a home or in a job where they belong and that's the kind of MAP where the main thing we are trying to do is relate the person to the setting.

This is a different kind of MAP. What we're trying to do is to see through your understanding in bringing these people together today what kind of MAP we want to draw of the territory that we don't have a very good chart for.

NARRATION continued:

Marsha: Many people ask what MAPS stands for. A MAP is a creative tool to help a person or an organization get to where they want to go. It's not an acronym. It's simply what any MAP does - it gives direction. (Note: Historically we used various acronyms for MAPS including McGill Action Planning System and Making Action Plans.)

WHAT IS THE STORY (HISTORY)?

Jack: Shafik is a human rights activist and community organizer in Philadelphia. He has been struggling with cancer for nearly twenty years. In this video segment he has gathered together a few friends, colleagues, and people who love and support him. The purpose is to create a jigsaw to put together all the pieces of the vision of his life.

TRANSCRIPT continued:

Shafik: Somewhere along the pike I felt I had a right to choose anything- to choose life, to choose friends, to choose family. I want to say that the people also gathered here with me are my chosen family: my wife Shina, who I intend to go deep into the future with; my most permanent sister Bahiya. We do not have the same mother or the same father, but she is my most permanent sister in stability. I asked Jack and Marsha to join me because they have become family that is unbelievable to me. They are people I know that if I needed anything and I made the call, that they would come. Things would be dropped and they would come. They know I would not make such a call unless it was a most just call.

Shina: Bahiya and I are a part of the village of Kumbaya in Philadelphia, which is our other circle of support in Philadelphia. Kumbaya in Swahili means come by here, and it is our pledge to come by one another when we need one another and to be supportive of one another at any cost at any risk. We see ourselves as a village of nine tribes. Some people see us as an organization of nine committees.

NARRATION continued:

Marsha: In this case, in Shafik's MAP, what you see is the dream, the nightmare and the history all intertwined and its up to the facilitator to really listen hard to get those pieces out. There have been times when Jack and I have been facilitating a MAP when we just couldn't get the history out. It is always a clue that something is going on underneath the surface and it is critical for the facilitator to keep probing to make sure we bring out that story because without the story you really don't have the MAP.

Jack: The facilitator has to create the safe place for the person to tell their story. You have to create an environment, you have to create an invitation so its OK for them to tell their story however they tell it Most people don't remember their stories with a strict chronology. You can put that in later, what you have to do is get the essence of the story, the milestones and meaningful bits.

Marsha: There's also a history to any organization so if you are doing an organizational MAP its exactly the same thing and the story of the organization when people come in, when people left is critical to getting into the next phases of the MAP.

TRANSCRIPT continued:

Shafik: A war came at me called cancer. It wiped me out for while and made me now understand that comfort was primary if I was going to continue my work. It was difficult to work with the amount of pain that I had in my body. It was difficult to be a part of people with the amount of pain that was in my head, in my spine, my left hip, my right shoulder. I realized if I was going to do anything else I would have to find a way to get comfortable.

NARRATION continued:

WHAT IS THE DREAM?

Jack: Linking of dreams and nightmares is universal wisdom and we've chosen the symbol of the dream catcher as an example of this. Within the dream catcher the webbing here snags nightmares which we all have, but we also have dreams and the dreams trickle through the gross webbing within the dream catcher and get caught in the feathers which are so delicate. Their delicacy is the secret of capturing and retaining our dreams. So too in life. This is the wheel of life. We have both dreams and nightmares and in the MAPS process we need to acknowledge both. Its not one or the other, its the two together that are required in a person's story.

Marsha: In this video, you see the merging in Shafik of the dream and the nightmare. In most MAPS the facilitator has to invite the dream and invite the nightmare and even in Shafik's MAP you'll see John make very discreet the difference between the dream and the nightmare.

TRANSCRIPT continued:

Shafik: The dream for me is in the very next chapter and are we talking about the next chapter. In this next chapter I want to see both of my sons, my oldest the seventeen year old Tahir to go into flight and sustain his flight. That he not be dependent but understand interdependence. And secondly for my youngest son Corey to be treated with full respect and be given the recognition of his great abilities outside of a special education classroom. Those are my dreams for the next chapter. I don't dream of anything in reference to Shina and I because its already written and established that we will be fine.

Bahiya: You said what you dream for Tahir and what you dream for Corey. What do you dream for yourself in this chapter?

Shafik: My dream is to be alive because that's not so certain, particularly with my cancer beginning to act up in several places on my body right now. I want to be alive, to keep growing, keep developing keep moving even while being radiated, even while taking chemotherapy. To not say "oh poor me" and stand still. But also not to be in denial. To be honest to what we believe. These are challenges that are to be confronted. If overcome move on, if not overcome slow down a little bit. If victory is not there that means defeat is there and the end of the story. I don't want us to be stuck again. I'm not denying I have major medical problems, health problems but I don't want to be stuck. I would feel defeated if I had to lay in my bed again for months or if I had to live in an institution like I did for seven months with strangers taking care of me.

In 1974 I had to live in an institution and I don't want to be there again. My dream is to sustain and build upon what we already have, to keep going, to keep moving to stay alive physically and ideologically, to keep new ideas flowing.

Jack: But if I heard it right in this community the chances of you going back to an institution are zero.

Shafik: Absolutely!

Jack: So in terms of being stronger and knowing that that's there, its there. That doesn't resolve it but some of the stress in past history is ancient history. We're beyond that.

Shafik: So I collapse or intertwine with the dream and nightmare.

NARRATION continued:

Jack: It's vital that one of the members of the facilitation team play back the dream, synthesize and summarize it. What you're doing is checking to see if its all there, checking to see if you actually got it right. Helpful things to do are to ask people if the colors are right, if the shapes are right. Whatever it is ask people to touch it. Because often people in the process of trying to remember have forgotten absolutely critical elements and as you play it back they'll suddenly blossom with a vital part that was either underplayed or totally left out. Play it back so it becomes theirs.

TRANSCRIPT continued:

John O'Brien: We have a funny sense of dream, because the dream contains the possibility of your death and we've put it in the dream circle and one of the ways that that possibility realizes itself in this chapter is a real clear focus on wanting to be sure that both Tahir and Corey have the best chance that they can to fly and to find their place.

NARRATION continued:

WHAT IS THE NIGHTMARE?

Marsha: The hardest question for facilitators to ask in a MAP is "What is your nightmare?". The reason people find this very hard to ask is that often they haven't faced their own dreams and nightmares. Without the nightmare there is no MAP. People ask us, "But can't we say 'what's your fear', or 'what's your biggest concern?'" Our answer is NO. We're using the word nightmare as in the dream catcher for a very important reason.

Jack: The nightmare actually grounds the whole MAP as it provides the foundation point because the ultimate purpose is that we want to move away from the nightmare and toward the dream. If we don't actually establish the nightmare and put boundaries around it we can't go on. We don't have to dwell on it, just give it a clear statement, put it out in the open, name it, then the MAP can proceed.

Marsha: A skilled facilitator always does this question quite quickly. Its not a matter of spending hours on it. It is stated and then we move on to the next part of the MAP.

Jack: It's uncomfortable for us and for any facilitator. You don't have to dwell on it, but you have to state it.

TRANSCRIPT continued:

Shafik: My nightmare is that I'd be alive in this chapter without life, that I cannot do everything I do right now - whether I'm missing an arm, whether I'm missing a leg. The only thing I'm concerned about losing is my mouth. I'm being very honest. If they have to amputate a leg or two, if they have to take an arm, I just want to be able to run my mouth, continue to talk and share all that is in my head. If I can't do that, my nightmare becomes real.

NARRATION continued:

WHO IS THE PERSON?

Marsha: The next question is who is the person or who is the organization. In a sense this begins part two of the MAP. The facilitator has already done the slugging hard work of getting through the dream, the nightmare and the story. And now we are saying who is this person. You want a rich portrait of the person or the organization. Sometimes we'll ask what do other people say about this person and get a whole list of labels. The purpose of this question is to get away from labels and to get into a description of who the person is. We say stay away from labels and jargon.

Jack: In the video segment on 'Who is Shafik?', Shina simply states "he's intense" and that's the truth, he is! It's a wonderful moment for he is intense and that's the kind of rich portrait we're really looking for.

Marsha: We don't want somebody saying the person is schizophrenic, the person is autistic, the person is severely and profoundly this or that label. Most labels don't give us any information on which to go into the future. Rule number one for the facilitator is to accept no jargon, no labels and to push for real words that describe a real person.

TRANSCRIPT continued:

Shina: He's intense, he's real intense, and sometimes his intensity is frightening. You know I would sometimes like him to be a little less intense. I know his intensity is because he is so committed to things and people. He has a saying, "I don't say things because I'm right, I say them because its what I feel." He feels with great intensity and it can be really scary.

NARRATION continued:

WHAT are the PERSON'S STRENGTHS, GIFTS and TALENTS?

Jack: We also like to take a second cut at who is this person by focusing on what are their gifts. What we want to know is what is the person really good at, what's unique, what's extraordinary about this person. Often we ignore some things that are absolutely spectacular about a person. What we are looking for here is what is that essence of the person that is often so simple we miss it - like friendliness, caring.

Marsha: The word here is also what does this person contribute. I like the word contribution when we're talking about gifts. I remember an example when we were working with some high school students. There was one student who was described by the adults as unable to do very much. They said she couldn't talk and she couldn't do this and she couldn't do that. The students however said "she's a great listener. She has a great smile, that's her contribution." We believe more and more in this day and age that being a good listener is truly a great gift but nobody had ever seen that before and it was one of those magic moments.

TRANSCRIPT continued:

Shina: I know that as far as the people in his life he is always going to give recognition to those people that he cares about, because that's who he is. He's going to always give, not just to people he cares about personally but to people in Nicaragua, in El Salvador, anywhere there is pain in the world. Where there is pain its a problem for him. He says, "As long as I'm comfortable and other people aren't, I'm going to always feel pain, because everybody should be comfortable not just me, not just my family, but everybody."

TRANSCRIPT continued:

WHAT SUPPORT DOES THE PERSON NEED TO ACHIEVE THEIR DREAM AND AVOID THEIR NIGHTMARE?

Marsha: At this point we get to the needs question and in revisiting the MAP we really switch this. Its not what does Shafik need to do. This now becomes the interdependence question. What do we all need to do together to help Shafik avoid his nightmare and get to his dream. The key word here is interdependence, not the Lone Ranger riding off into the sunset, but a circle of friends a group of people interdependently figuring out what to do in fairly complex situations.

Jack: What we want to avoid are some of the traps we slipped into before, where people actually ended up at this point bureaucratizing the MAP and creating a list of what somebody else needed to do. What we really want is to help this person achieve their dream, avoid their nightmare, explore their gifts, and to be the best they possibly can be. The focus is what do we have to do together interdependently to help the person or organization achieve their dream and avoid their nightmare - that's the key question and the key point of the exercise.

Marsha: The essence of the MAP is that together any group, any family is better than any one person alone. The line "together we're better" leaps out at us at this point in the MAP.

TRANSCRIPT continued:

Shafik: Obviously I need to pay attention, better attention to my health. To take a time out, every now and a then, to pay a little bit of attention to the demon radiation. I need to acknowledge that when I feel pain I should feel pain, not try to cover it. Feel it, deal with it, toss it.

Shina: One of his friends once told him put yourself on your agenda. I like to remind him to reiterate what she said, to remind him to do that, to "put yourself on your agenda". He is like that, and I know there are times when I give him reason to be intense. I know those are some of the things that I need to give attention to and recognition to as well. Those are things I would say are really important.

NARRATION continued:

WHAT IS THE PLAN OF ACTION?

Marsha: The final question in the MAPS process is now what are we going to do, what is our plan of action? If we have done a really good job facilitating the process we have this rich tapestry of information and the Plan of Action leaps right out at us. It's usually right there and we often hear people say, why didn't we see that before. The reason we didn't see it before is that we didn't have all the relevant information collected.

Jack: Occasionally what happens is even with all that information we still can't see the end. In those instances what we've done is developed a second tool called PATH. PATH is a precise tool designed to cut through even the most complex problems and get us to a structured plan of action.

But in most MAPS we now have the information and we know what to do. The facilitators task now is to get everybody committed to who is going to do what, when, and where. We want to be sure that everybody is locked into their commitment. Everyone also needs somebody who agrees to be a coach and remind them to do what they said they would do. The aim is for participants to deliver on their commitment to the Plan of Action.

TRANSCRIPT continued:

John O'Brien: Some level of harassment of you about paying some attention to yourself is probably a real contribution to your ability to do that. Yeah, so live with it, is the message. Get used to it, they've got to live with a lot of intensity. You've got to live with their loving you and wanting you to survive and having an idea about how that happens that's different than yours.

We've also got some work to do in terms of some sense of a future for the village and for African Voices Alliance and particularly and something we can begin to attend to within the next couple of days is kind of an initial PATH, that's not how does Corey get to school but how do we join together to make sure that Corey has the opportunity to be as influential in Philadelphia as his father.

Jack: Whew!

Marsha: I like that.

Jack: That's some people's nightmare.

FINAL COMMENTS:

Marsha: In summary and for all of the people that want to be facilitators we basically have
one rule and three guidelines.

The **one rule** is very simple, its **the golden rule**, its the golden rule of MAPS.
Don't do a MAP to other people unless you have experienced a MAP on yourself, on your own family. Unless you've gone through the dreaming and listening don't do this to others. Because unless you're vulnerable yourself, particularly to the dreams and the nightmares you can't ask another person to do what you haven't done.

Now the guidelines; the **first guideline** is:
ask all the questions.

Jack: What you have to do is ask all the questions not most of the questions - all the questions. You can be creative with the order of the questions because people will mix and match. But as a facilitator you have to listen for all of them, play them back, and be sure all that content is in then you have a full MAP that's what we're looking for.

Marsha: The **second guideline** is:
use a graphic.

Jack: We use a graphic because it turns on a whole other part of your brain. As the graphic recorder creates the images of the dream and the nightmare and the story something happens with people. They are able to see the whole portrait and a whole other reality emerges. The graphic turns on another part of our own reality. A graphic is not an incidental part of the MAP. It is critical, it is the essence of the MAP. A MAP without a graphic is NOT a MAP!

Marsha: And the **final guideline** is:
have co-facilitation.

Jack: Co-facilitation means two, not one - don't do it alone.
There's many reasons for this. There's safety in numbers
you won't get into hot water if you have a team. We are
trying to model teamwork on everything. Co-facilitation is
an answer.

The last thing we want to do on a MAP is to get closure
and the simplest way to do this is to have final words,
final images from all the participants. And so that is what
we are about to do on Shafik's MAP.

TRANSCRIPT continued:

Bahiya: This has been really good for me because its really focused
me in a way that discussions are hard to do. Its focused in
on the things that are key and on what the next directions
need to be.

Jack: A lot of stuff is going to happen and we'll deal with the rest
because we're really powerful together.

Marsha: I'm amazed at the clarity that I think we have in terms of
direction.

Shina: Its been wonderful for me to be able to see his past , our
past and also see our now to see it visually in front of me
in colors - its just beautiful.

Shafik: Now to me what we've done here is complete. I need then
to simply say in reference to what is out of the room is my
mentor Judith Snow who taught me something very fabulous
that I would never forget and never fail to say and that is
while waking up is an end to sleep, waking up does not
have to end your dream.

JUDITH SNOW ON DREAMING

Dreaming is a process of communication in which all human beings participate. In our culture dreaming is not well understood but through the MAPS Process it is possible to really understand that dreaming will tell you exactly where a person needs to go in their life, and also what it is they have to contribute along the way to the people in their lives.

In other words if we become good at listening to what a person's dream is, we become good at supporting them to find their way to that dream.

Many cultures have understood dreaming as an essential part of being a human being. In those cultures people often spend time sitting around just talking to one other about what it is they would like to do in their lives. But in our Western culture, most dreaming is done through a process of fantasy.

For example, for many years I had the fantasy that I would love to be a truck driver. My truck was a high tech truck, one of these very large, more than the eighteen wheelers, that has a bed in the back so you don't have to stop on the road. The purpose of my truck was to drive from Toronto to California. I would get lots of money for doing this. I'd work for 6 months of the year and make enough money to take off for the rest of the year.

The second six months I would rest and reflect and do other things. I used to be embarrassed about this fantasy because obviously I'm not really going to be a truck driver. But over the years I have met a number of people who don't use words and they began to teach me to really pay attention to what I was dreaming about. They taught me that they could really communicate with other people even though they weren't using words. I began to look for where this communication coming from.

I finally got over my embarrassment about my fantasy and began to tell it to other people. I have a very strong support circle and my circle listened to my dream. What we figured out was that my dream had these important seeds in it. The seeds are that my work is very important to me, that I wanted to get around, and in fact I wanted to get around the whole continent as part of my work. I want to be bring something to people that is very important. I want to make enough money by doing my work that I can spend time at home resting, reflecting, and learning other things to bring to people.

I now do travel internationally talking to people about how we can support all of our diversities.

My point is we all have gifts to contribute to each other and society. My dream has come true and my life is satisfying to me. It is a life of contribution to other people. All the information we needed was in the dream about my being a truck driver.

What does this have to do with MAPS. In the MAPS Process we listen to the person's dream. We listen with ears that don't say, "Oh this very unrealistic, this could never come true." We listen with ears that are searching out the themes of life that are important to this person.

We need to ask what do these themes mean to that person. What are some of the ways we can have these seeds planted in our community right now . This is where the other side of the dreaming comes to reality because in the seeds of the dream are the ideas about what are the gifts that this person has to contribute to other people.

The problem with most kinds of planning around people who are vulnerable, either because they are labelled physically, behaviourally and or mentally disabled, is that we focus on what's wrong with the person or with their family. As we focus on what's wrong with them, we end up with ways to try and fix them but with no way to move forward in that person's life. Often you end up getting stuck.

With MAPS we're not looking at what's wrong with the person, what we're looking at is what is it that this person has to contribute to other people in his or her community. What are the gifts that this person has that the community needs and that if the community has it will grow richer and grow stronger.

The dream has in it the seeds of the person's gifts. In my truck drivers' dream, my getting around and giving things to other people is an important part of my gift. In fulfilling that gift I actually employ other people, because I hire five other people to help me get around the country. I use a van,

I'm paying repairs on the van and I'm buying the van.

I also use airline tickets, so I'm keeping the airlines in business like thousands of other people. Those are part of my gifts, those are part of my contributions to other people. In the dream what we will always find is something about any person that will be a real contribution to other people. It's often something that is simple but its a solid beginning.

Many people will disclose that their gift is that they really like to make other people happy. If we use that gift then we have somebody who is going to be a really great generator of relationships in the community.

Whatever the gift we then have the opportunity to sit down together in the circle of the MAPS process and say okay how can we use these gifts, these particular gifts in the community.

Inclusion is Not Exclusion
Marsha Forest   Dec. 1994

Inclusion is
the future.

Inclusion is
belonging to one race,
the human race.
Inclusion is
a basic human right.
Inclusion is
struggling
to figure out
how to live with one another.

Inclusion is not
something you do
to someone or
for someone.
It is something we do
WITH
one another.
Inclusion is
not a person.
"the inclusion kid."
Not a program.
Not an adjective.
Not an add on.
Inclusion is
a noun.

Inclusion is
not something we do a little of.
It either is or isn't.
It is not a fad.
Not a bandwagon.
It is a trend,
similar to democracy.
"With liberty and justice for all."
All means all.
No but's about it!

Inclusion
is the opposite of exclusion.
Inclusion is not exclusion.

Inclusion is fair play,
common sense,
common decency,
hard work.

Inclusion is elegant in its simplicity
and like love
awesome in its complexity.

Inclusion is a battle cry,
a parents cry,
a child's cry to be
welcomed, embraced,
cherished, prized,
loved as a gift,
as a wonder,
a treasure.

Inclusion is
not spending more money on
building more prisons,
mental hospitals,
nursing homes,
group homes,
but investing in
real homes,
real life,
real people
all people.

Inclusion is
pain
struggle
joy
tears
grief
mourning
celebration!

Inclusion is the ship that isn't even built yet.
It is a new ship.
One we will build together.

Inclusion is like a good jazz combo,
like an orchestra
disciplined to play melody
in harmony.
Inclusion is
a kaleidoscope of diversity .
bits of color, sounds, shapes, sizes.

Inclusion is
The future.

What is Person Centred Planning

Marsha Forest, Jack Pearpoint & John O'Brien

Many people are asking "What is Person Centered Planning?" Basically, it is a constellation of tools developed to help a person or a family who want to make a purposeful and meaningful change in their life. Person Centered Planning tools include Individual Service Design, Lifestyle Planning, Personal Futures Planning, Essential Lifestyle Planning, and MAPS and PATH.

Person Centered Planning is a wonderfully clear three word name. No jargon. Very straightforward. The planning is centered on the person. Simple and yet profound. The planning is not for the convenience of the service, the organization, or even the family (when a person not a family is the focus). The plan simply serves the hopes, dreams and visions of the focus person or family. This is very exciting work.

Is it easy? No. Does it always work? No. A plan is simply that: moving from 'hope' for a better future to the specifying personal commitments that increase the chances of moving toward that future. There are no guarantees, only person-to-person commitments. But the plan gives motion to the possibility that something real and meaningful will happen. A good plan with no action won't take anyone anywhere.

The facilitator is a servant to both the person and the process. Imagine the facilitator holding a set of empty containers and drawing the contents to fill each container out of the person and his/her friends, family and colleagues. Each of the different tools offers a somewhat different set of containers.

The choice of method is more like choosing a musical instrument than it is like selecting a hammer or a screwdriver from a toolbox. Facilitators learn a method that matches their gifts; they practice faithfully; they take master classes; they carefully review their performance. Some facilitators, like some musicians, learn more than one instrument as a way to extend their range or deepen their skills in their chosen instrument.

The plan does not belong to a service organization or to the facilitator. Both the process and the content belong to the person and those who are committed to accompany the person along the journey the plan outlines.

The facilitator gives up any preconceived notions of what is possible or impossible, even what is good or bad. The facilitator is not passive but pushy about the process of getting clear statements and clear agreements about which direction the person wants to move and which route the person wants to take. The facilitator is never pushy about content: where to go and how to get there is up to the person and the person's allies. This takes practice. It's easy to stop the plan from truly belonging to the focus person by standing in judgment. The only limits on what the plan can include are the limits of imagination and commitment. The only limits on what the planners can achieve are the limits of their ability to enroll and align the necessary resources.

Some people ask, "What if a person makes a bad or illegal choice?" Others wonder what to do if the person asks for the moon. Both of these questions result from the same misunderstanding; both assume that the process belongs somehow to the facilitator. But it doesn't. The process offers people a way to clarify what they want and what they are willing to work together to make happen. Those who know and care about the person, and often those who control necessary resources, need to choose to sign up to help the person. The process offers a way for people to surface and negotiate disagreements about what is right and what they will consent to work on.

Of course, facilitators are responsible for their own ethics and can always say no before beginning to process to helping someone who wants to take a wrong direction like planning a crack selling business or putting someone in an institution. Even in such challenging circumstances, it may be helpful to 'listen under' the 'named goal' before outright rejection, because it may turn out to be the only available term for deeper and richer dreams and goals.

These tools are for all people; not just for people with disabilities. We find that the more facilitators use the tools in their own lives, the less dangerous they are. Dangerous facilitators impose their own words, their own images and their own interpretations on the focus person.

Good facilitators are good listeners who see their role as creatively helping people to design lives that reflect their gifts. That's what Person Centered Planning is really all about.

Before you work with others, do these introductory activities.

Introductory MAPS learning checklist

I have…

_____ Watched the Shafik's MAP video.

Read…

_____ All my life's a circle, pp.1-28

_____ Action for inclusion

_____ What's really worth doing

_____ From behind the piano

_____ Answered the sequence of MAPS questions reflectively, for myself, with facilitation, and provided the facilitator/ recorder with feedback.

_____ Facilitated another person in answering the MAPS questions, and received feedback on my facilitation.

_____ Made a graphic record of another person answering the MAPS questions and received feedback on my recording.

_____ Developed a set of notes for myself on "What I want to review before I facilitate a MAP."

_____ Made agreements with at least 2 other people who will support my practice with MAPS by encouraging me and debriefing with me.

_____ Identified a family I will approach to be my partners in taking the next step by allowing me to facilitate a MAP with them.

Introductory PATH learning checklist

I have…

_____ Watched the Introductory PATH training video.

Read...

_____ All my life's a circle, pp.29-43

_____ PATH Workbook

_____ Been a PATHfinder on an issue that matters to me, and provided the facilitator and recorder with feedback i.e. have had my own PATH done.

_____ Facilitated another person's PATH, and received feedback on my facilitation.

_____ Acted as a graphic recorder for another person's PATH and received feedback on my recording.

_____ Developed a set of notes for myself on "What I want to review before I facilitate or record a PATH."

_____ Made agreements with at least 2 other people who will support my practice with PATH by encouraging me and debriefing with me.

_____ Identified a person or group I will approach to be my partners in taking the next step by allowing me to facilitate/ record a PATH with them.

by O'Brien, Forest, Pearpoint

MAPS and PATH
Differences & Similarities

Jack Pearpoint, John O'Brien & Marsha Forest

Maps and PATH are creative Person Centered Planning tools designed to identify do-able action steps in the direction of desirable futures.

They are only two of many excellent tools. Good facilitators have a full tool belt, and, as they approach a situation, they make judgments about which tools are most appropriate. Good facilitators may even switch tools in mid-stream when new information shows that the initial selection won't help people get where they want to go.

Both Maps and Path can be used with a person, a family, or an organization. Both need welcoming locations and include the people who support the person in focus or the key actors in the organization. Both get to specific next steps. Both use coaching and graphic facilitation.

The major difference between the tools is their starting focus. The center point of the MAPS process is the "story" of the person or organization at the center. MAPS encourages people to tell their story; to create a rich portrait of their journey which includes a statement of both a dream and a nightmare. By nurturing the dream, and confronting the nightmare, people increase clarity on a desirable future direction. Next we create a full positive portrait which brings strengths into clear focus before moving to define next steps.

In most cases, when we hear the story, we discover that there are obvious beginning action steps right in front of us - so close we couldn't see them. Thus, the MAP supports a journey to a desirable future - with a coach.

The MAPS process is ideal to get to know a person or organization. Sometimes its important to get to know someone who is a newcomer. Sometimes it is important to make sense when identity and direction seem to be lost or confused. MAPS is much more powerful and revealing than file cabinets full of data because the story 'makes sense' of all the isolated facts: they fit into the pattern of a life.

If a person or a team is mired in a deep, complex or painful situation, MAPS may not be a good tool. If people have struggled endlessly, revisiting the past may simply irritate open wounds. Generally, organizational situations are multi-layered and the past may be too complex for a quick overview. These are times when it may be appropriate to consider PATH as the tool of choice.

PATH emerged from our own frustration with the MAPS process in complex situations. We needed a 'sharper' tool to cut through and get into action in spite of complexity. PATH is razor sharp and must be used with caution.

PATH moves people through a highly defined set of questions. It is 'pushy' as a process, though it does not push toward any particular answers. PATH sets the 'confusions' of the present aside for a time, creates the opportunity to investigate common values, and then travels into the future. Through "planning backwards," PATHfinders create vivid images expressing their dream. Next, we come closer to the present, (still remaining in the future) and invent possible and positive goals that we will have 'accomplished' one year hence. In carefully orchestrated steps, the PATH process then 'grounds' the PATH with a brief visit to the "present", then systematically reviews who will be needed (enrollment) and what we will need to do to be strong enough to sustain this journey. Changing direction, and noticing both our goals and our enrollment needs, we again plan backwards from the future until we arrive at immediate next steps to be taken - with a coach.

In both MAPS and PATH, the process gets to next steps - with a coach. In both, team facilitation provides one layer of safety. Since both tools are person centered, the individual controls the depth and intensity of the process. They have the right to stop or to persevere. There is a simple safety check available to all facilitators; ask the focus person how it is going. They will tell you. Listen. A helpful guideline is 'do no harm'.

Choosing the right tool is an art. Make a great tool collection, then practice, practice, practice. Facilitation is an art, but it can be learned. Renewing dreams is a great gift, and with MAPS and PATH, people leave ready to take steps in the direction of their dreams.

What is Inclusion?
Shafik Asante

In 1955 the story of a brave and tired woman named Rosa Parks was put in front of this country's awareness. They say this woman got tired, in fact, historically tired of being denied equality. She wanted to be included in society in a full way, something which was denied people labeled as "black" people! So Rosa Parks sat down on a bus in a section reserved for "white" people. When Rosa was told to go the "her place" at the back of the bus, she refused to move, was arrested, and history was challenged and changed. All of this happened because Rosa Parks was tired, historically tired of being excluded. She had sat down and thereby stood up for inclusion!

Another powerful cry for "inclusion" is being heard today. This new cry is being raised by people with **unrecognized abilities**, (the so-called "**dis**abled"). Many people whose abilities are regularly denied or ignored feel that society is not honoring the right to participate in society in a full way. Part of the call is for better accessibility, such as more wheelchair ramps, more signs and materials in Braille, community living, etc. The Americans with Disabilities Act represents and attempt to hear the "inclusion" cry. However, much more needs to be done including a search for an acceptable definition and practice of inclusion.

Across this country a definition of inclusion is offered. It is generally accepted that "Inclusion" means inviting those who have been historically locked out to "come in". This well-intentioned meaning must be strengthened. A weakness of this definition is evident. Who has the authority or right to "invite" others in? And how did the "inviters" get in? Finally, who is doing the excluding?

It is time we both recognize and accept that we are all born "in"! No one has the right to invite others in! It definitely becomes our responsibility as a society to remove all barriers which uphold exclusion since none of us have the authority to "invite" others "in"! So what is inclusion? Inclusion is recognizing our universal "oneness" and interdependence. Inclusion is recognizing that we are "one" even though we are not the "same". The act of inclusion means fighting against exclusion and all of the social diseases exclusion gives birth to - i.e. racism, sexism, handicapism, etc. Fighting for inclusion also involves assuring that all support systems are available to those who need such support. Providing and maintaining support systems is a civic responsibility, not a favor. We were all born "in". Society will immediately improve at the point we honor this truth!!

New African Voices Alliance (NAVA)
403th N. 54th St.
Philadelphia, PA 19139-1422
Tel: 215-472-4204 Fax: 215-472-9323
For permission to reprint, call NAVA or Inclusion Press @ 416-658-5363

It is with great sadness that we report the death of our friend and colleague, Shafik Asante on Sept. 5, 1997.

There are No Disabled People

Shafik Asante

Throughout the entire history of the U.S. there have been unrecognized people. Unrecognized people are people who are looked upon as being valueless. Such people were even vilified, or criminalized. American Indians, the only original Americans, were seen by the early settlers as having no value, thus major attempts were made to rid society of "these people" (who are still referred to as savages in the U.S. Constitution), and their land was stolen from them. Eventually millions of people were stolen from Africa to work this stolen land, and these people also were eventually declared valueless became acceptable. Yes, other societies have done this as well, such as Hitler's Germany to name one. Hitlers' first target were people he saw as the "disabled".

There is an ongoing debate in society now about how to address the issue of disability rights. The issue of rights is also not a new conversation in the U.S.. As a result of African people in the U.S. (so called "blacks") being seen as valueless, unabled, etc., a civil rights/human rights movement was forced to emerge. As we know, this movement was led by people who felt locked out, unwelcomed and thus excluded from the "American Dream". In fact many of these excluded people experienced the "American Dream" as an "American Nightmare", and said so! This movement was the most powerful movement for inclusion that our society has ever witnessed. A people only seen as unabled clearly demonstrated their abilities, and society was forever changed.

Today yet another group of people are looking for the dream of life, liberty, and the pursuit of happiness. And again the obstacles of exclusion has been put in place. Again labels have been used so as to justify the exclusion and overbearing isolation of 'these people"! Who are they? They are the people know as the "disabled"!

There are many of us today who believe that one of the major obstacles to all of us recognizing our "oneness" (even though we are not the same), is that we label others as well as allowing ourselves to be labeled. Think for a moment of labels we've placed on others. In almost every case the label has been used to put someone down, to separate ourselves from "them"! And we label people so as to appear different from, or better than the "others".

A term used today that we believe needs to be re-examined and eventually discarded, is the term "disabled"! Why? Because there are no such human beings. Disabled, like the other term "handicapped" gives us a major misconception of the people who are forced to wear this label. Fortunately millions have moved away from that 16th century term "the handicapped". Let's remember that this term was used to portray people who were missing limbs on their bodies as people who only sat around with their caps in their hands begging. It was perceived that such people could do nothing else but beg. They were seen as valueless.

The term "disabled" also implies unableness, can't do-ness. Think of what it means to **dis**-regard, to **dis**-respect, to **dis**-card. Ask the younger generation today what the term "dis" means. They'll tell you it means to ignore, or to abuse in some way or another. To disavow means to not recognize, or to not take responsibility for. **Dis**card, **dis**ease (not at ease), **dis**own, **dis**trust, **dis**order all imply negativity. So do we want to emphasize what people can't do, their disability; or what they can do, their ability, their ableness!

Many new voices are encouraging us to realize that we aren't really talking about people with disabilities or the so-called "disabled". We must move to acknowledging that we are more often than not talking about people with "**Unrecognized Abilities**"! Only mechanical devices can get disabled, or something without life. But there is no human being who is unable to do something. Yes, we all have various limitations but no human is disabled. It's just that their abilities are not sought out, are not recognized.

Others are saying "So what's the big deal. What's all the fuss about what we call them?" We need to remember, that how we refer to a people has a lot to do with how we also treat them. The early Africans were labeled "slave" thereby justifying their inhumane treatment. The original Americans were called "savages" not people. Again a label is used to disregard a peoples' beauty and value. We say there are no disabled people, only people with **unrecognized abilities**!

© 1994 Inclusion Press with
New African Voices Alliance (NAVA)
403th N. 54th St.
Philadelphia, PA 19139-1422   Tel: 215-472-4204 Fax: 215-472-9323
For permission to reprint, call NAVA or Inclusion Press @ 416-658-5363

It is with great sadness that we report the death of our friend and colleague, Shafik Asante on Sept. 5, 1997.

Joel and Bryce: A Lesson in Friendship

Marsha Forest and Jack Pearpoint

Often great discoveries appear to happen as if by magic. An inventor has the "aha!" experience. The great singer becomes an overnight sensation. Stop. Look deeper. The "aha!" of the inventor happens in one instant - **after** years of study, and thousands of failed trials and experiments. One day it all comes together - as if by magic - into something we call electricity, or the telephone or the microchip.

Similarly, the overnight singing sensation in fact has toiled for years, practised endlessly, invested untotaled dollars on lessons, and then, one day if she is fortunate, the 'break' comes. She has done all the unseen hard work, and then is at the right place, at the right time and has found the right songs and the right manager. Is that "magic?"

So it was at the first Toronto Summer Institute on Diversity, Inclusion and Community in July, 1996. 110 people gathered to learn from each other about the how to build inclusive schools and communities. While we "talked" about building inclusion and strengthening relationships, the real thing unfolded right in front of our eyes. The "aha" was watching two children have 'fun' and form a friendship - while we talked. We were given a powerful and moving reminder of wisdom we already knew. When the hard work has been done and the conditions are welcoming, we can make friends with each other in our daily lives.

Inclusion Defined

Inclusion, by our definition, means learning to live with one another. It is not simply being **"in"** a physical space. It is being **"with"** and embracing the people in that space. The prerequisite is 'being there': being at the table, in the classroom, in the workplace. Tragically, for all too many, exclusion is still the norm. They are not even 'in'. Doors are closed on the basis of race, sex, sexual preference, social class, ability, and disability. In these cases, the battle is to get through the door, over the threshold, to sit at the table. This is no mean feat, but it is the first step.

Once 'in the door', subtle exclusion often still exists. We often carry the walls of exclusion with us into the new spaces we call inclusive. We drag our institutional mentalities with us into schools and communities - and call it "inclusion" and "community living." We congratulate ourselves when we succeed in moving people out of overtly walled institutions (and it is a necessary step). We forget that the most debilitating barriers that need to be moved are the attitudinal walls within our own heads. Until we move them, we can make minor and positive adjustments, but we will not actually "include" people. Like Joshua at Jericho, we need a movement to smash the walls (physically and mentally) and get those old walls to "come tumbling down!"

At the new Toronto Summer Institute,

we decided to embark on a bold journey by breaking down walls and creating a new way of doing our work. It wasn't easy giving up the old walls. They felt comfortable and gave a sense of security. But we chose to "go to the edge, and fly". It wasn't all scripted; it wasn't all neat and tidy. We did have a clear vision and a plan to build a beacon that might focus us on the right questions and avoid more exercises in futility.

We planned to invite those we usually omit. To make this institute unique and transformational for the majority of the 110 participants, we knew that including some of the "normally excluded" was a key ingredient. We knew that our 'inclusive' choice would increase frustration for the minority who wanted the definitive **answer, the recipe.** But, we 'let go' of the illusion of control. Everyone would have the opportunity to learn in time - or not, if they chose. We focused on the 100 who were struggling to "live the questions."

> *Be patient to all that is unsolved*
> *in your heart...*
> *Try to love the questions themselves*
> *like locked rooms and like books*
> *that are written in a very foreign tongue.*
> *Do not now seek the answers,*
> *which cannot be given you*
> *because you would not be able to live them.*
> *And the point is, live everything.*
> *Live the questions now.*
> *Perhaps you will then gradually, without*
> *noticing it,*
> *live along some distant day into the answer.*
> -Rainer Maria Rilke

Our group of 110 was a microcosm of inclusive community - a community of capacity. The entire ethos of the physical space conveyed the 'new'. We turned down free but dingy classrooms - with little cubicles to do our own things. Instead, we found a beautiful airy space where we all stayed together in two large rooms. It radiated with natural light. There were stunning views of the city and Lake Ontario from the 23rd floor penthouse, and plenty of space if one wanted to just daydream. We know physical atmosphere is an enormous asset or deterrent to learning. Physical geography shapes (but not controls) the capacities for growth in a group. Where we can make it work for us, it is worth the effort. We did, and the group exploded with learning.

We didn't overdo the decor. We know the power of first impressions, so we made it welcoming. But for our community, we did not want to "control" it's evolution. We wanted it to emerge and take on the personality and values of the group. The co-learning hosts (core faculty team) gave up ego and control. We chose not to overdose with major lectures. Instead, we all did short content modules, and left two thirds of the total time to respond to the capacities and needs of the group - to be together, to talk to one another, to make connections, and to build what we call a "learning marketplace".

We had diversity. We worked hard to ensure that we had diversity. This is a key. A conference where everyone is 22, an "A" student and from Toronto may be interesting, but it cannot have the richness and depth that emerges when the age range is from 8 to 64 and there are professionals, families, people with interesting labels and people from a variety of social classes. In our community, Alfredo, a Spanish speaking bus driver and parent of a child with a disability from El Paso, Texas sat next to a Professor from Detroit and a 14 year old from Toronto. The conditions were set for real interaction and real learning to happen. Inclusion, creativity, new ideas, do not and cannot flourish when the participants in any group are uni-dimensional - a conference

Texas (June, 1996). A bond was built and an invitation was extended to come to Toronto.

People saying 'yes' to the seemingly impossible increases the potential for creativity and new life to happen. Janet and Daryl found out about the institute late. They did not have the funds to attend. They had never taken Bryce, who uses a wheel chair and is labeled profoundly disabled, on an airplane. They had never been out of the USA with Bryce. They had never eaten bagels and lox.

We said, "If you can get to Toronto i.e. raise the money for the airfare, we will find money for the tuition and housing for you with Shafik in our neighbourhood. We will arrange transportation, oxygen in case of medical emergency, and we will feed you bagels and lox."

They said 'yes' and arrived in Toronto on July 5, 1996.

Other important factors. In Texas, Bryce fell in love with Jack, now known affectionately as "Uncle Jack". They played together in the swimming pool in the incredibly hot Dallas June sun. It is not talking about friendship or inclusion that really forges people together. Doing things together starts the process. The Thomas family sat and ate with us for two days in Texas. That was the start. Was there a guarantee that things would go further? No. Invitations are

of all families, all children, all ex-offenders, or all professors, etc. Diversity creates the possibility for creativity to flourish. (Note: there are some occasions when uni-dimensional gatherings are more powerful - such as with Alcoholics Anonymous, Narcotics Anonymous and various therapeutic and self-help gatherings.)

Joel and Bryce

The magic happened in microcosm in the relationship that developed between Joel Hollands who is 12 years old and came to the Institute on our invitation as a student helper. He was there to help us with whatever needed to be done and to participate in the day to day (and night to night) events of the institute. This was the contract. Full participation.

Bryce Thomas, 9 years old, was there with his parents Janet and Daryl. They just moved to Texas from Louisiana. They had met Shafik Asante at a conference and were inspired by his message that inclusion was bigger than disability. They also met Marsha and Jack at the Southwest Institute in Dallas, made often, but many of us are unwilling or unable to risk saying 'yes' to new opportunities. 'No' is most common. Knowing when to say 'yes' and 'no' makes a difference.

While Bryce and Jack were swimming in the pool with Judith Snow, Jay Klein, and Marsha Forest, fun was the key. We weren't thinking about inclusion, diversity, disability, community. We were having a ball, outdoing one another with splashing, games, etc. Bryce, who doesn't speak very clearly yet, was shouting "I like this Jack. Do it again." A very tired Jack limped from the pool sunburned and exhausted an hour later.

Janet, Bryce's energetic mom and advocate, had the chance for a few precious moments to just sit and watch. She even disappeared for a few minutes as she sensed she could trust this lunatic bunch of pool crazies with her precious child.

So the Thomas family decided to come to Toronto to be with some people they liked and trusted, and who seemed to genuinely like them in return. No one felt sorry for them or their son. This was a comfortable group of people who challenged themselves and each other, and had fun as well as doing some serious work.

On Friday evening, Bryce, Janet and Daryl were sitting on our back porch in Toronto, eating again and testing the delicacies of the Jewish community - bagels, lox and herring. Janet and Daryl tasted everything tentatively. Bryce, usually on a diet of puréed baby food, actually ate lox (smoked salmon). The child proved to be the adventuresome type with champagne tastes in expensive delicacies.

And so the conditions were ripe for inclusion to begin. Children and adults were coming and going. The phone was ringing. People were thrilled to meet each other. There were people in wheelchairs, and people who walked. There were people who spoke with words, and those who spoke without. There were children and there were adults.

The conditions were set for the magic to happen.

What occurred was not magic at all. Conditions were brought together to create the possibility for lives to be lived to the full. Exploring this vast human potential is what we want for all our children and for ourselves - for everyone.

Joel and Bryce on the Institute...
We interviewed Joel Hollands and Bryce Thomas about their experiences at the Institute. Their remarks are profound in their simplicity. (Note: Joel was interviewed by phone and Bryce by e-mail with his mother typing his answers.)

With Joel...

Marsha (M): Joel, you mentioned that John McKnight's opening talk at the institute really struck you. What particularly stood out for you?

Joel (J): I liked the part about a glass being seen as half full or half empty. Our society is concerned with what is wrong with people - the empty part. I just never thought of it like that, but it's really true. Nobody ever pays attention to the full half of the glass.

M: Is this true at school for you?

J: It's true especially at school. Nobody really seems to care about anybody else but themselves. They are all judging people all the time. You know the saying, "You can't judge a book by its cover." But that's what they do at school. Everybody is just judging all the time. If the adults see someone with a problem, they assume an empty glass and don't see the full side. They assume its all empty and there's nothing good there.

M: Why do you think this happens? Is there anyone taking leadership?

J. There's no one there to set an example. There's no direction about that sort of thing.

M: About what sort of thing?

J: About values and attitudes.

M: Let's talk about you and Bryce. What do you think happened that brought you two together. After all Corey and Jonathan were there too, but you and Bryce really hit it off.

J: The second night of the Institute, me and Jonathan and Corey were playing ball at our house. Janet (Bryce's Mom) had to go somewhere for a few minutes. She asked us to watch Bryce while she was gone. That's what happened. We played together.

M: Tell me a bit more. What drew you to each other?

J: He likes the same super-heroes that I like. Batman and Robin. Bryce liked to talk about Batman, Robin and the bad guys on the roof. So we shot balls to the roof and had a good time.

With Bryce...

M: *What happened that made you and Joel become friends?*

Bryce: (B) *We liked each other and our ages are close.*

M: *What did you especially like about Joel?*

B: *He is nice.*

M: *What do you think Joel really liked about you?*

B: *I was nice to him.*

With Joel...

M: Joel, how did you understand what Bryce was saying? Lots of people can't seem to understand him.

J: At first I had trouble, but Janet would sort of tell me what he was talking about, and once I understood what the subject was, I knew what he was talking about - like the "bad guys on the roof." We liked playing the same games.

M: What role did the adults around play in all this.

J: They were great. They weren't discouraging but were encouraging. I really learned a lot from the adults at the institute. I learned about stuff going on all over the world. I even talked to Te [Ripowai] a lot about New Zealand and Heather about Scotland. Everyone was really friendly and getting along with one another.
You all had no barriers for me and Bryce. You didn't say "You can't do this and you can't do that." Also nobody told me anything bad about Bryce.

M: Joel, what would happen if Bryce came to your school.

J: He wouldn't be allowed to come.

M: OK. Let's assume he was finally allowed to come to your school. What do you think would happen?

J: They, the teachers would ignore him. They wouldn't deal with him and they'd talk about him behind his back.

M: Joel, why do you think Bryce liked you?

J: That's a good question. We like to do the same things. We really weren't all that different from one another. We like animals, the same kinds of movies, Batman and Uncle Jack!

M: What did you like best about Bryce?

J: He listened to what I had to say. It wasn't like one of us was controlling each other. At school groups of kids stay together because one is popular and usually one controls things. You stay together just to fit in.

M: Joel am I right to say that Bryce really seemed to like you just for you.

J: That's it. That's right. He liked me for who I am and I liked him for who he is.

And Bryce said...

M: *What did you like most at the Summer Institute?*

B: *It was fun. It had elevators to go down and up.*

M: *Do you want to come back next summer? Why?*

B: *Yes. Because I like Joel.*

M: *Do you have any suggestions on how we could improve the work we do?*

B: *I want people to let Joel and me be crime fighters and do karate.*

Janet, Bryce's mom adds: Bryce talks about Joel all the time. In fact, with all the friends and relatives we've been visiting recently, the first things Bryce says are:

"I went to Canada. I found a friend. His name is Joel. We are crime fighters."

Back to Joel...

M: Joel, what do you think Bryce would like more of at home in Texas and at school.

J: He says he wants to play more and be more with the other kids.

M: Does he have friends at home?

J: Whenever we talked about that he wouldn't answer. He'd change the subject.

M: If you were going to talk to a group of adults, mostly teachers or other professionals, what would you tell them?

J: I'd say that even though Bryce needs a good education, he needs just as good or at least the same amount of being with other kids and having more friends. That is just as important as his education.

M: How do the kids at your school who don't have friends act.

J: They act weird. Nobody ever gives them a second chance. Most of them are very smart but they don't do their work and they get in lots of fights. The more they are excluded the sadder and sadder they get and they stick to themselves.

M: Is there anything else you want to add.

J: You all (the leaders) were more like friends than teachers. At school the teachers act like they see each other every day but they don't know each other. You all acted more like....(long pause)

M: Joel take your time. It sounds like what you want to say is important.

J: It is but I just don't know the words. You all (Marsha, Jack, Te Ripowai, John, John, Judith, Shafik) you all were like a ..... (long pause)..like a family. You acted more like you act with your own family. You didn't always agree but you liked one another and I wish it was like that at school.

Joy and Sorrow

We are moved by Joel's innocent wisdom. We read his words with both joy and sorrow. Our joy is that we created an Institute in Toronto that allowed Bryce and Joel to touch each others lives, and Janet and Daryl to see the great potential in their son - and that he could experience friendship.

We feel joy for Dave and Cathy Hollands as they saw a side of their son Joel that often gets clouded because he too has trouble at a school that won't recognize his unique gifts with people.

Will this relationship continue? The boys live thousands of miles apart. But there are phones and there is e mail. Already plans are underway for next year in Toronto. Equally important, both boys have experienced a new and intense friendship. With this as a foundation, they will continue that search. It is the opening of a possibility that didn't exist before.

This is not the story of a bright child befriending a poor pathetic handicapped kid. It is the story of two boys whose hearts met. They liked to play together. They listened to one another. They found acceptance in one another's eyes. It is Joel who now avidly waits for e-mail and is sorely disappointed when it doesn't arrive. Bryce was so excited when we all called the other night that he didn't let anyone else get a word in edgewise. He was literally choking with excitement. It is a two way street - a reciprocal relationship where each benefits by knowing the other.

This is also the story of several families that have made connections that benefit and stretches them all — the Hollands', the Forest-Pearpoints, the Asantes and the Thomas's. The story has just begun. Many lives have been touched by the friendship of two children. A spark has been ignited.

Some final points.

Several points need to be clarified. We believe that neither Bryce nor Joel are unique or unusual. Neither the Hollands family nor the Thomas family are endowed with "special" powers. It is too easy to write this off as one of those 'special' happenings. It was extraordinary (and we celebrate that), but in its foundation - it was very ordinary. We believe in our hearts and souls that what happened with Bryce and Joel, and with all our families together, can happen anywhere and everywhere. It takes hard work, but it can happen. It is not a miracle.

Several **conditions** are needed **for friendship and learning** to flourish in families, in schools, in workplaces, in communities.

- An **atmosphere** of welcome, **hospitality** and trust.
- A **Belief** that Bryce has as much a **right to be present** and participating as Joel. We must believe that Bryce is as valuable and worthwhile as Joel.
- A **Belief** that there are millions of Joels and Bryces in **every neighbourhood** anywhere in the world.
- **Role Models** set the tone and model the very behaviour we want to see in the children. It will not happen otherwise.
- People (including adults and children) must **sit with one another, share meals**, conversation and connect with one another before anything can develop.
- **Safety boundaries** are established for children.
- **Children's names** - and no other labels or negative descriptors - are used.
- **No jargon** is necessary. Plain

language will do.

- Complex **medical briefings** are **not required** for friendships. Joel had all his questions simply answered by those who knew and loved Bryce. He needed to be around Janet, Daryl and others who loved and accepted Bryce. He needed to know what he wanted to know and no more. He didn't need fancy explanations about cerebral palsy. He wasn't interested. He was interested in Bryce as a person.

- When we **focus on community capacity**, communities will develop their own internal capacity to facilitate inclusion.

- **Attendants** and assistants are necessary when needed for **physical care**, but this must not get in the way of friendships developing. Stepping out of the way so a relationship can happen is a critical skill.

- Adults present must know how to **foster and facilitate friendships** and community for **all** - and when and how to 'step back'.

- **Financial resources** are needed. Note: what happened with Joel and Bryce involved no extraordinary financial resources.

- We need to **acknowledge** and **act** on the fact that **young people** - Joel and Bryce - and **their families** are the key to the **future**.

- **Schools must involve families and neighbours** in figuring out how to live day to day together at school. Professionals must be hired who are trained and skilled in facilitating relationships among **All** children.

The Emperor is Naked...

Our writing is controversial. It was never popular to point out the king's nudity. But here we are. We are not asking people to agree or disagree, but rather to stop and consider what we are saying.

Joel and Bryce taught us what we already knew about relationships, but needed to be reinforced/reminded. When we lock out either Joel or Bryce from one another's gifts, we are unwitting participants in a system that values profit over people and still sees some as more valuable and important than others. It is a system that is hurting many people - if we are willing to look past all the marketing hype and through the "sheer" 'garments' of administrative control and 'professional' cover-up. We need excellence and professionalism. However, too often we see mounds of marketing hype, of obsolescent 'products' that have no educational value - beyond making massive profits. Too often the 'tools' have become expensive excuses for not looking truth in the face, for not facing every child and asking the simple question, "what do we need to do to help you become a full participating citizen?"

As publishers we get reams of papers and books across our desk about adapting the curriculum, about fostering relationships, about how to do this and how to do that. "The emperor is naked". Most of these tomes are a waste of good trees. Most are focused on measuring how empty the glass is, and how to plug the leaks. They give simplistic recipes for mythological children who do not exist. Each child comes to us at school with unique gifts. Our view is that all children are glasses half full - not half empty. That is our focus. We must find tools to mine and polish whatever gems each child brings. There are no pat answers of how to assist Bryce in school. There are collaborative strategies that pull the creativity of groups of people together - in teams. Groups of people who know Bryce need to sit, dream and plan together. There is no manual for this. It does take skilled people with good tools and time to build action plans based on the heart. Such plans will need continuous revisiting and revision. Paradoxically, the criticism of such ideas is that they take too much time. Meanwhile, if we actually tally the massive time wasting committed to bureaucratic form filling - and meetings, we could implement meaningful planning tools for every child, involve the untapped talents and energies of families and fellow students - and thus turn crisis to opportunity. Is it impossible, or is it just that some of us are frightened of change.

Montessori said it. Pestallozzi said it. Rousseau said it. Rudolf Steiner said it. A.S. Neil said it. Dewey said it. All the giants in education observed the same thing. Children are great and natural learners. Unfortunately, with all our needs for 'structure' and control, we stop them from learning. We shut down creativity systematically. We ask the wrong questions, demand answers that we already know, and thus create schools that are seldom places of delight, creativity, learning and joy. Too often our schools breed boredom, pain and unhappiness.

We need to tell the truth when we see it. We need to say that indeed the emperor is naked. Most of the curriculum and planning tools we "dress" our systems in are fluff - they are not really there. We have been sold a very expensive bill of goods, and all of us are too frightened to say - we are naked. Meanwhile, the cost is being calculated in "lost futures" for our children. We need to take heart. We need the wisdom of a little child who had the courage to tell the truth - 'the emperor is naked'. We need to get back to our hearts. We need to invite families to help us with the things we don't know. We need to admit we don't know it all and learn

together. We need to admit that children can often teach us what to do as they are not yet tainted by the fear of disability that we see. All is not lost - there is time to begin afresh.

Our friend and colleague Rose Galati chilled 110 people to the bone when she introduced us to her two teenage daughters Maria and Felicia. Rose put on a pair of rubber gloves. With passion and power in her voice, she told of how adult assistants feed her daughter Maria as she sits in her wheelchair in the cafeteria. The adults wear rubber gloves. They obey the regulations. No children are nearby. No wonder. We are teaching them that Maria is untouchable - dangerous. We will all be infected/afflicted unless we wear protective 'gloves' - or just stay away. Some rules need to be broken if we are going to change the world so all children - and all adults can be welcomed.

Rose flung off those rubber gloves and cried with heartfelt passion- "NO MORE!" Ironically, her children attend a Catholic school. And the words in the 'religion classes' pale beside the powerful lessons being taught to our children by our actions. What are the ethics we want to teach our children?

Is our fear of death and mortality so intense that we need to protect ourselves and our young from the faces of life. Rose recently nursed her dying father and was not afraid to clean and feed him. Her daughters have taught her well what life is all about. Maria was once institutionalized. So was Bryce. So will we all be as we grow older if we do not stop the insanity of segregation and the hiding of pain.

We need to read more about philosophy and art and creativity. We don't need manuals to tell us how to include people. We know how. It is not a matter of how. It is a matter of "will we do it"? Will we make the effort? Will we change? Once we say we will, all we need are teams and circles of people who really care and who want to change the world. The rest is too often a diversion, another protective layer preventing change, - a waste of time, money and effort.

The data is in. We know that all human beings first and foremost need to be needed and loved in order to live. Children in foster care and orphanages suffer most pain not because they are not adequately cared for and fed, but because they are not loved. It is as complex and simple as that.

Let us not be afraid to talk about what really matters. Let us be bold and together talk about love. Let us weed those people out of the lives of children who care more about preserving the status quo, more about their jobs, and more about their pensions than about the lives of children.

We know all this, and we know you know all this, but it took Bryce and Joel to remind us of the beauty and simplicity of what can happen in an atmosphere of love and learning.

Building inclusive communities and relationships is a simple profound concept, but not an easy task. It will take spiritual and financial resources. Probably, we will not see the kinds of communities we dream of in our lifetime. But remember that things do change: Nelson Mandela is the President of South Africa; Palestine is a recognized state; women are increasingly seen as full human beings; and Bryce and Joel are friends. This is indeed a powerful beginning.

As in the parable of the "star fish" where a person is walking along the beach and throwing star fish back in the ocean one by one, we may not save every single 'starfish', but for those that we do, it sure makes a difference.

The best and most beautiful things in the world
cannot be seen or touched...
but are felt in the heart.
Helen Keller

Listen to the Children:
Hope was Ignited:

Marsha Forest and Jack Pearpoint

We are always amazed at the quality and sensitivity of suggestions made by children when we are called into a school to find solutions to complex issues. This is still "novel" to most educators who still seek "expert" solutions from "professionals" when the real experts are sitting right in front of them.

If we had only one suggestion to make to all educators, it would be: "**ask and listen to the children**". We are not saying that adults don't have good ideas. We are not suggesting turning everything over to the children. We are not abrogating responsibility, avoiding discipline or inviting anarchy. We are saying let's add their voices to the list of those we listen to. We added a clarification - to ask AND to listen. We need to do both.

We find that children often bring a fresh and unique perspective to quite complex problems. Their heads are less cluttered with "can't" than most of us, and often they have the audacity to state the obvious and simple truths we are too close to see.

We were in a Ontario school attempting to work with family, staff and students to build a quality educational experience for all children - including a beautiful child named Lorna. At seven years old, Lorna was on the verge of expulsion. Her crime - pulling hair. Her labels - too many to mention. They were a lovely family with a beautiful and complex child. Everyone was frazzled and frantic as their seven year old was on the verge of suspension based on the school's "zero tolerance for violence" policy.

This is an extraordinary example of the kind of insanity making behaviour in some schools today. To equate bringing a hand gun to school with "hair pulling" by a child with the label autism is a policy to create violence - from families to administrators. It is beyond reason. We acknowledge that pulling hair causes a minor disturbance. But to equate this with life threatening violence is truly theatre of the absurd. But the principal was adamant. Lorna was "violent." The policy was the law. There could be no exceptions. The solution was suspension and expulsion.

Picture this violent child. Big eyes, small frame, sings and hums, has many friends among the other children. This is not a gun-totting gangster. (Even if she was, we have to come up with creative and constructive solutions to this issue as well.)

We gathered a group of about thirty children from the school and asked the principal and staff to sit and listen to their children for an hour. We invited Lorna's family to participate when appropriate. Her grade 2 teacher and supportive assistant joined. Lorna was in the middle. Most of the children crowded around on cushions and on the floor.

We started chatting with the children about friends and friendship in general - not about Lorna at all. We used the metaphor of a glass half-full or half-empty. The children liked that. Some felt the glass was half full. Others argued it was half empty. It was lively. The children were enthralled. We asked the children what their "gifts" were. We drew a big gift graphic. Lorna was just one of the circle of children.

"How would you feel if you had no friends?" we asked the group.

Words emerged as they do all over the world. Their words were: sad, lonely, not good, bored, need to get friends, left out, frustrated, humiliated.

Our next question was, "What would you do if you had no friends?" Their answers: I'd kick, be unhappy, be mad, do nothing, cry, skip school....and the key that always comes out "I'd kill myself." In our experience, this answer is universal when asked of children age 10 and over. Without dwelling on the fact that loneliness kills, the children genuinely understand how unthinkable loneliness is. We moved on.

"What can we do to make and be friends with one another?" Their answers: go swimming together, go to the movies, call each other, go places together, hang out together, play together.

We explained our belief that we all need help in life. "What are some examples of things you need some extra help with? Their answers: reading, painting, basketball, spelling, crafts, to stop hurting myself, writing, talking louder, drawing, math. One child spontaneously volunteered that his grandma needed help walking, speaking and hearing.

We then asked Lorna if we could focus on her for a few minutes. She gave us the OK sign. At times she said "I'm itchy" and then went to the nearby piano which she played quietly. It was not disruptive. Later she returned to the center of the circle with her assistant and several children who sat and held her hands. Her parents joined her in the front of the room.

With her parents surrounding Lorna, we urged the children to ask anything they wanted to know about Lorna and her family. We assured the students they were free to ask anything.

Clearly magic was happening. Jack was recording everything in colourful graphics. When the recess bell rang, no one moved. The children decided unanimously to stay. The principal, surprised at the whole development, went and got his camera.

At the appropriate time, we asked the children if they had specific suggestions about how Lorna could be more a part of the class. They were bursting with suggestions. We had a good age range of children - not simply from Lorna's class. This really made for a lively discussion.

Lorna's dad was often speechless and close to tears as he heard the children's desire to include his daughter.

* * * * * * * * * *

At the end of the session, the teachers commented that the children had devised a better Individualized Education Plan (IEP) than they had. They were not defensive, but were enthralled with the quality of the responses generated by the children.

Lorna's mom and dad thanked everyone and planned a future session - with pizza for the kids. They were both too emotional to talk. They summed it all up in a letter.

"Watching the children today was a remarkable experience for us. Doing the PATH and then following it up with the amazing discussion with the children has given us hope again for the future. In just a few hours Lorna became connected to the school and the children in a new way. The staff finally broke down their "professional" reserve and came to a place of real understanding of our vision and hopes for our two daughters. Hearing the children express such love and acceptance of Lorna was truly inspiring."

The North Star Dream

We now think about our "North Star" every day. In our family's North Star, Lorna is a full citizen in our community. She lives in a lovely little cottage type house right near our home. She has a "funky" roommate - a theatre person/ artist from our local and thriving theatre community. She is supporting herself through her skills in art. She feels she is a valued contributing member of the community.

She has mastered new ways of communicating. She uses the phone to call us. We can go away for vacations and not feel tied down and worried all the time.

Lorna has links to a nearby farm where she keeps a horse. She has pets in her home. Her church community has also fully welcomed her. She is happy and content because she has many friends with whom she does numerous activities. When she sees former teachers and mentors on the streets, she tells them, "Thanks, you really made a difference in my life."

This is a transcript of the North Star part of

the PATH we did. It was the first time Lorna's parents (both extremely articulate) had stated out loud their deepest hopes for their daughter. The father, was deeply touched by the experience.

Following Up...

We did a follow up call several months later to see how everyone was doing. We are thrilled to report that Lorna and her family are not only doing well, they are in their own words "doing great!" The is a verbatim report from an emotional dad on what happened.

"That day was the breaking point. They were either going to finally understand, or we were going to fight them legally and spiritually. The whole day was very moving. I still get really choked up talking or trying to write about it. The process was very moving. Hope was ignited.

We are moving toward our North Star and we are right on track with our one year goals. I can't believe it. The principal is even relaxed. Lorna says "good morning" to him each day and he actually smiles.

We just got Lorna's report card which says she is making good progress in all areas - especially in controlling her behaviour. She participates more in everything and is getting used to changes in routine. She can count from 1-50 and is learning addition facts. She has improved self-control and is making gains socially and academically."

Lorna's dad was thrilled to report that Lorna had signed her own report card, and that as a family, they were all doing much better than in the fall.

"There is no more tension or upset with the school. We are enroute to the North Star."

Instead of a war, this situation was saved when everyone involved sat together; listened to one another; and listened to the children. It would have been a tragic waste of time, energy and money to have taken the other route. More important, Lorna would have been excluded - perhaps beginning the long slide to institutionalization. No school system should ever expend the energy and finances to exclude children when we know that creative solutions can be found. It is a matter of will - and priorities. The same energy is available to welcome all children - or to battle endlessly for exclusion. Congratulations to Lorna, her family and their school. It wasn't easy, but they are on the right path.

Defining Problems Differently

Since the major "problem" defined by the principal and special education teacher was Lorna's "disruptive" behaviour (specifically pulling other children's hair) we addressed the issue head on.

"What do you think Lorna needs some help with?" Their answers:
* talking and listening to us
* looking at people when they talk and when she talks
* eating her lunch
* learning to be a friend and how to
* learning to play with the other kids
* expressing her feelings
* controlling her emotions and not pulling hair

Why do you think she pulls other children's hair?
* She wants to communicate.
* She wants to get to know us.
* She doesn't know it's wrong, she wants to get our attention.
* She wants to say "hi".
* She likes to smell and feel hair and she doesn't know it hurts when she does it.
* I don't think she likes to pull hair. She just doesn't know how to control it.

What can we do to help her?
* When she reaches out to pull hair just hold her hand and gently but firmly say "No". (We acted this one out a few times.)
* Don't ever slap or hurt her.
* We can talk to her more.
* We can care about her more.

The children asked a lot of great questions of Lorna's mom and dad. They would have gone on all day but we were all emotionally drained.

Circles, MAPS and PATH: Creative Tools for Change

Marsha Forest, Jack Pearpoint &
Judith Snow

Warning Label: Circles, MAPS and PATH are NOT programs. They are powerful tools for change. They are part of a tool box of person centered planning strategies. Each of these processes must be engaged in on a voluntary basis in order to be effective and not to be harmful. The ethic of the tools requires that the facilitators have had the personal experience of being the focus of these powerful strategies in their own lives. In other words, *"Do No Harm"*. Do not use these tools with others until you have experienced them for your own life.

Circle of Friends/Circles of Support

What is a Circle? Circles do not belong to any one author. They are an ancient concept of building community and relationships in a modern context. Sometimes a Circle is called a *Circle of Friends*, other times it is referred to as a *Circle of Support*. A Circle is a group of people who gather around a person who has become excluded or isolated. The focus of the group is to find and create ways for the vulnerable person to participate in her/his community. This participation will be structured around the gifts and talents that this person wants to contribute to community.

The circle discovers these gifts by *listening to the person's dream* and personal story. Historically, circles have often been built around people who have been labeled disabled and who have become trapped in the human service system or other forms of isolation. However, circles are change tools and are applicable to anyone of any age who is vulnerable, isolated, or in crisis. Circles

usually originate around the needs of one individual, but over time, circles diminish dependency and foster reciprocal, respectful relationships for all.

A circle is not a program. It is not a one shot exercise. It is not a quick fix. It is a way of being with a person. It is a form of being *members of each other*.

For more information on why and how to create circles see these materials:

Books:
Circle of Friends by Bob Perske and Martha Perske (Abingdon Press)
From Behind the Piano by Jack Pearpoint (Inclusion Press)
What's Really Worth Doing by Judith Snow (Inclusion Press)
Members of Each Other by John O'Brien and Connie Lyle O'Brien (Inclusion Press)

Videos:
It's About Friendship (Vision TV - available from Inclusion Press)
Friends of Clubs (available from Inclusion Press)
Dreamcatchers (available from Inclusion Press)
With A Little Help From My Friends (Inclusion Press)
Kids Belong Together (Inclusion Press)

MAPS (Making Action Plans)

Developed by Marsha Forest, Jack Pearpoint,
Judith Snow and John O'Brien

MAPS is a powerful way of creating a holistic portrait and of collecting real information about a person, a family or an organization. **MAPS** is a process for people or organizations to share their stories and begin making changes that will lead to closer relationships with vulnerable persons, families, or in organizations. The process is based on an intimate reflection of a personal story (history) - the story of a person who has lived through crisis, a family that has shared difficult times with a vulnerable person, an organization/team struggling with change.

The eight questions in the **MAPS** mandela lead the group through a focused reflection on the gifts and capacities that are so often hidden. The questions help the group to reflect on the valuable contribution that everyone can make. The outcome identifies ways that the community can draw together to support all people to be full participants.

A MAP is not an IPP. It is not a case conference. It is not an assessment tool. It is personal. It is designed to be co-facilitated. It uses a colourful wall graphic and visual imagery. It can be used with any age group. It is specifically designed to hand over "leadership" to people who have been isolated (and the people who are most intimately involved with that person or family). It is a tool to empower those with voices we seldom hear to be leaders in planing their own lives. It enables those in "support" roles to be genuinely supportive of an individuals' own priorities.

For more information on **MAPS**:
Books:
   All My Life's a Circle (Inclusion Press)
   Inclusion Papers (Inclusion Press)
   Action for Inclusion (Inclusion Press)
Videos:
   The MAPS Training Video (Shafik's MAP) (Inclusion Press)
   Miller's MAP (Inclusion Press)
   With A Little Help From My Friends (Part 3 May's MAP) (Inclusion Press)
   Kids Belong Together (Inclusion Press)

PATH
(Planning Alternative Tomorrow's With Hope)
developed by John O'Brien, Jack Pearpoint, and Marsha Forest

PATH is a systematic creative planning tool that begins by creating a vision, then specifies actions to get moving on the Journey to that desirable future.

PATH is a powerful tool. It makes the implicit - explicit. It takes out the "whining" and asks bluntly if people are willing to do the hard work to invent their future.

PATH plans backwards. It begins by creating a Future Dream (North Star), then focuses on creating a real positive and possible future.

PATH is a tool - adaptable to individual, family or organization situations (large and small). **PATH** relies on the creative tension set up by exploring the future and contrasting it with the present (Now). **PATH** produces a step-by-step grounded action plan which locks in individual commitments and enrolls other important actors. The Final Step is the "First Step" which begins **immediately.** If Pathfinders are truly committed to moving towards **their** dream (North Star), an enthusiastic action plan emerges which begins now.

PATH is not for the faint of heart as it truly asks "do you want to make change happen?"

PATH is not easy. **PATH** is powerful, challenging and real. It is an action oriented, colorful, co-facilitated plan of action.

For more information on **PATH**:
Books:
The PATH Workbook (Inclusion Press)
All My Life's a Circle (Inclusion Press)
Videos:
The PATH Training Video (Joe's Path) (Inclusion Press)
The PATH Demonstration Video - a School Team Planning (Inclusion Press)

For information about training events and materials:
Inclusion Press International
24 Thome Crescent,
Toronto, ONT.   M6H 2S5   Canada
Tel: 416-658-5363
Fax: 416-658-5067
web page http://inclusion.com
E-mail: 74640.1124@compuserve.com

LIFE IS EITHER A DARING ADVENTURE OR NOTHING AT ALL!

CIRCLES, MAPS and PATH:
Three Creative Tools for Change

Marsha Forest and Jack Pearpoint

This chapter is about three creative tools that have been used internationally to assist people with disabilities and organizations dealing with disability issues to move into more **possible and possible futures**. The tools are dynamic, creative, colourful and have high impact on both the individuals and organizations using them. The tools are Circles of Support (Friends), MAPS (Making Action Plans) and PATH (Planning Alternative Tomorrow's with Hope).

In this article we will describe the philosophy, the common elements and the differences in these three tools and how we have used them in the field of adult services. The tools are cross cultural in application and have been used widely in North America (Canada and the United States), England, Scotland and Wales and as well in New Zealand and Australia.

Circles, MAPS and PATH broadly come under the heading of personal futures planning. Simply this means the person is at the heart and soul of each tool. We use the famous Maori quote to sum up the philosophy of these three tools:

"What is the greatest and most precious thing in the world?
I say to you.
Tis people. Tis people. Tis people."

In these planning tools, the **person** is first and foremost - the heart of the matter. In order to actually realize what any person needs and/or wants, nothing is more important than genuinely **listening** to that person. We must not "presume" wants or needs, rather we must help an individual make choices, and then facilitate their journey towards those goals. It means **giving up control**, and learning how to **listen**. It means being non-judgmental, but creating a positive supporting framework within which there is a balance of **safety** and **responsibility**, all focused by genuine selection of direction by the person. Our "planning" **for** others needs to mature to **"planning with"**, and always needs to be within the framework of what that person wants for his/her life. It is vital to remember that it is **their** life. Striking this balance is not always easy, in fact it is hardly ever easy, but it is always **right.** There are also no guarantees that the person will get what they want, but at least, we have done our best, and there is integrity in the route we have tried. It is honest. There is one additional reason to go this route. Very often it works!

Belief System

The belief system underlying these tools is that **all** human beings are more alike than different. We share common basic needs: to be loved, to belong, to have meaning, to have fun, to have dignity and respect in all aspects of life.

We believe there are **no "them" and "us"** people. There is simply **WE. We is all of us.** All of humanity. The key is "we".

There is absolutely no difference in the essence of what all human beings want. We use this wonderful poem by the writer Mayer Shevin from Syracuse, New York the anchor for our work.

Language of Us/Them
Mayer Shevin

We like things
  They fixate on objects
We try to make friends
  They display attention
  seeking behaviour
We take breaks
  They display off task behavior
We stand up for ourselves
  They are non-compliant
We have hobbies
  They self-stim
We choose our friends wisely
  They display poor peer
  socialization
We persevere
  They perseverate
We love people
  They have dependencies
  on people
We go for a walk
  They run away
We insist
  They tantrum
We change our minds
  They are disoriented and have
  short attention spans
We have talents
  They have splinter skills
We are human
  They are ... ?

*Mayer Shevin is an advocate/writer
from Syracuse, N.Y.*

The Golden Rule

The driving force behind Circles, MAPS and PATH is the ethic of the Golden Rule. This sounds simple, but is profound and difficult in its application. The first application of the principle begins now. We ask everyone reading this chapter to not practice these tools on anyone else until you have gone through the exercises yourself. Practice them on your self, your family, your friends. Experiencing the vulnerability of putting your own life on the line is a safety valve. You will have deep respect for the power of these tools. It takes enormous courage to dream, to share one's personal nightmares, to tell your own story (history). Facing our devils and angels is an awesome experience. It is not easy. It is however transformational. That is what matters. Circles, MAPS and PATH are tools that get to the heart of the matter. They are not superficial or time wasting. They can help anyone who really wants to do the hard work of getting on the journey to **their** destination.

These planning tools are designed to start a journey of discovery for any person of any age and ability. The tools are powerful therefore need trained, humble, patient and skilled facilitators. The ability to speak verbally is also not a constraint. Using all forms of augmentative or facilitated communicating is excellent. Age is no boundary. We have found that the older the people, the more challenging the task, but age is NO barrier, nor is level of disability. It may take longer for people with limited life experiences, people we incarcerated in institutions or group homes, etc., to figure out where they want to go, but longer is not a limitation.

Working with Circles, MAPS and PATH, we have had to give up the notion of disability, labels, and jargon. We ask ourselves, as we ask you, to base your work on the most cutting edge research on how people learn. Let go of the past. Move into a new future. Labels only hide and mask our ignorance of what is really going on. Descriptions and action plans based on reality help us move into the future.

If an individual has medical problems, we get them medical attention. We are not throwing out the baby with the bath water. We support good science and medicine. However, once medical conditions are sorted, we focus on the full life of the person living in a community. These action planning tools move us back into communities brimming with hospitality and the "ordinariness" we all have and crave so desperately in our daily lives.

We constantly remember that **loneliness** and **lack of belonging** are the **major killers** of people with disability labels (as well as our elder citizens). Thus, we begin our work with the first tool - Circles of Support, designed to look deeply at who surrounds any person labeled disabled.

The Circle of Support Exercise

It is important to remember that this is an exercise and not an outcome. In the past, people have confused the exercise with the actual building of Circles which is a life long practice. (see From Behind the Piano, Pearpoint and What's Really Worth Doing, Snow.) The Circle exercise is a powerful consciousness raising tool to **start** a process that might lead to building relationships in anyone's life. The exercise provides a framework for discussion and action. It allows us to clarify what is really important in a persons life, and focus on where to begin. Random action without direction can be dangerous to people's health. Medical professionals diagnose before they treat. The Circles exercise "checks out" one of the most common and critical problems facing many humans - loneliness and disconnectedness (lack of belonging).

We suggest reflective music accompany this exercise - preferably a tape or CD with one instrument i.e. a flute, violin, piano. The music sets a tone and creates a feeling of safety. With the right music playing, it gives permission to pause, to think, to have a reflective silence

without "filling every space with words". We remind people that this is a self reflective exercise about the life of the human service workers themselves. Do this for YOU. It is not about someone else.

The Circle of (Support) Friends Exercise
Draw 4 circles on a blank sheet of paper.

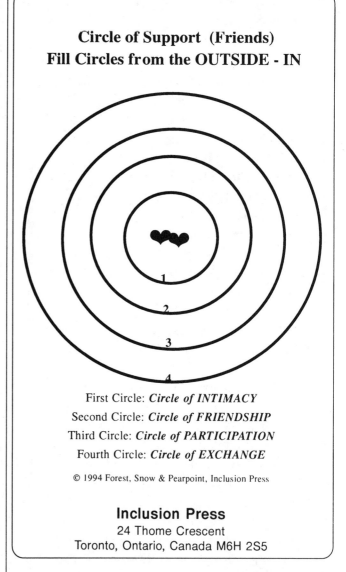

Circle of Support (Friends)
Fill Circles from the OUTSIDE - IN

First Circle: *Circle of INTIMACY*
Second Circle: *Circle of FRIENDSHIP*
Third Circle: *Circle of PARTICIPATION*
Fourth Circle: *Circle of EXCHANGE*

© 1994 Forest, Snow & Pearpoint, Inclusion Press

Inclusion Press
24 Thome Crescent
Toronto, Ontario, Canada M6H 2S5

Circle #1 - The Circle of Intimacy
Put yourself in the middle, then in the first circle, put the names of those people who are essential to your life. People you would have a hard time imagining being

without. These are the people closest to you. This is usually a small number. It can include people who have passed away. Some have put God, a pet or a favorite book in this circle. There is no right or wrong answer. It is whatever you want. In New Zealand's Maori community this always involves whanua (extended family).

Circle #2 - The Circle of Friends

In the second circle put the people who are defined by you as "friends". They didn't quite make it into the first (intimacy) circle, but they are close friends or relatives. This circle is **usually** bigger than the first circle.

Circle #3 - The Circle of Participation, Association, Networks.

In the third circle, write in places you go to be with people, groups you belong to, work or church groups, sports, clubs, etc. The circle of participation is where you **DO** things and have encounters with other people.

Circle #4 - The Circle of Exchange.

In this circle put all the people you pay to be in your life. Lawyers, doctors, beauticians, plumbers, the storekeeper. This is usually quite full of people for everyone. For "clients" of the human service system, it is packed.

Take a good look at your circles. What have you learned about yourself from doing this? Is there anything that jumps out at you? Is there any action you might consider to change the **pattern** of relationships in your circles? (Note that there is no correct number of people in each circle - other than the number that is correct for you.)

Now Do It Again...

This time, we ask people to think of one person they work with who has a disability label and who lives in a residential situation. We ask them to fill in the circles for that person. (Note: You can't actually "do" someone else's circles, but you can make a good guess for the purposes of comparison.)

We have done this all over the world and the outcomes are universal. Most of us have a fairly healthy network of friends and relationships. However, for adults living in the human service sector, the picture almost always looks "empty" (see diagram 2) with the outer circle of exchange full to brimming, and the inner circles virtually empty.

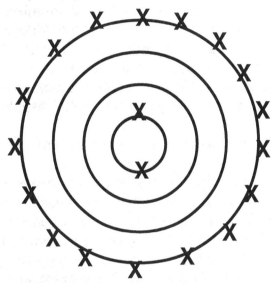

Now **ask** the **two key questions** that focus our thinking on what we have done to people with disabilities, and why. We ask everyone - including human service workers, *"If your life looked like this how would you feel?"* (diagram 2) The answers are universal from the Atlantic to the Pacific. Common words are *lonely, isolated, sad, bad, depressed, anxious, horrible.* The second and more profound question is. *"What would you do? How would you act?"* This also elicits universal responses, especially from human service workers. *"I'd cry, I'd withdraw, I'd reach out for more people, I'd act out."*

But when we ask the people who are the recipients of the services what they would do, they have one universal answer instantaneously:

I'd commit suicide.
I'd die.

Teenagers and people with labels are very clear without any hesitation. We all know this. But the answer is too painful for most of us to face head on. As human service professionals, we are helpers, fixers, doers. We genuinely want to help, to connect people, to make them less lonely. Stop! First, we must wait, listen and hear their pain. We must let them state their reality, regardless of how painful it is for us to hear. We must listen to their truth, that death is preferable to being alone. Then and only then can we can move ahead. We know the "bottom line'. We know what is really important.

What We Have Learned:
Fill Circle Three - From the Outside In

We have a strategy to begin the healing process. It is **not** filling circle one and two. We do not have the power to "create intimacy". Rather, fill circle three. **Participate! Join things! Do things** together! Asking people to be friends based on being nice, or even worse, on pity or charity, is doomed to early failure. No one wins.

We **can ask** people to enter into relationships based on shared interests - the magic spark of mutuality and respect. We have learned to ask a wonderfully simple question that hopefully starts the connections. *"What do YOU Really Like Doing?"*

What Do You Really Like Doing?

Ask anyone "what do you **really** love to do? Where do you like to go? What are your hobbies, interests? Unless someone is dead, they can and usually will tell you what they like to do. It is delightful to see a person blossom, especially people who were there all along - but we never knew, because **we never really asked**. We are always fascinated by what we learn about all people when we ask this fundamental question. It is the foundation of building communities of capacity.

Of course the skeptics will say, "but the people I work with"

a. can't speak
b. are too low functioning
c. are too behaviorally challenged
d. are not ready
e. are too old, too young, too fat, too thin etc. etc. ad excuseum

Let us review the basic core foundation beliefs of CIRCLES, MAPS and PATH, and get rid of the excuses. We believe:

1. **ALL means ALL!** (What part of all don't you understand?)
2. Anyone living and breathing (including with a respirator) can (with a little help from their friends) figure out what they really want to do.
3. People who don't speak (out loud) need the most creative facilitators to help assemble the puzzle of what the person really wants and is interested in.
4. If we actually **ASK** people, they will tell us what they are interested in, not what they think we want to hear. (Note the **attitude** of the **asker** often determines the quality of the answer.)
5. All necessary supports must be provided as a basic human right! i.e. wheelchairs, hearing aids, any technology that assists. (We aren't talking BMW's here, just the basic life supports that are necessary for daily living as human beings in a just society.
6. **Together We Are Better.** No one can figure this 'stuff' out alone and in isolation.
7. **It takes a whole village to raise a child.**

Circles on the Spot:

Circles are not some "abstract fluff". They can be used in real time to struggle with real issues. Two types of occasions are common. The first is when there is a group already gathered and there is an "opportunity" to welcome a newcomer. A Second common opportunity is when people are organized specifically to explore building support around a person. On such occasions, getting the right people invited is half the battle. A short story makes the point.

Elaine: An Example of Possibility (Circles on the Fly)

Elaine is 33 years old and has just moved into an apartment for the first time in her life with two other thirty-something working women in a middle sized Canadian city. Elaine is scared. She still works at the sheltered workshop but is looking forward to finding supported employment within the next six months.

If there is an opportunity to "welcome" a stranger - a new person - (everyone is gathered) a good facilitator can do a Mini-Circle on the spot. It involves the facilitator asking "Elaine" to join her and then having a short public conversation with Elaine. That conversation begins with the facilitator telling a little about herself - what she is really interested in. Example: *"I (facilitator) love to cook - especially Asian food; I am a mad roller blader, and I am a movie nut. I really enjoy the wild chase scenes in movies like "Speed" and stuff... I know they're terrible, but I love the distraction."*

Then the facilitator asks Elaine the million dollar question.

"What do you like to do?"
Silence. We wait. More silence. Then Elaine speaks,
"I like the theatre, I like movies, I like men."
This is a good start. "
What kind of theatre and movies," we probe.
"Funny stuff, stuff I can laugh at," she answers.
"And what kind of men. "
"Any kind."
We all laugh. A personality starts to peep through the cloud of former silence.

Then comes the key to this whole exercise. The facilitator (the community connector, the bridge builder, the circle #4 worker) asks the people in the community around Elaine,
"Who would like to get together for coffee with Elaine to talk this over."

A date is set. A time boundary is set (say two hours).

Note: This is not a time for "approximations". This is about commitments. But the commitment is to "go for coffee" - not solve all the world's problems. These boundaries create a safety zone that allows people to say "yes". It also pushes us to be clear. Some people would be delighted to go for coffee - but they have other commitments. We cannot afford to have them say "yes" and then NOT show up. That breaks the trust.

Having asked for volunteers, the facilitator must now wait and pray. In all our years of asking, people have always responded positively. Never (and we mean never) - not in Dublin, Christchurch, Brisbane, Toronto, or Glasgow has no one volunteered. It was scary at times, but the community capacity emerges if we wait and show our trust in the inherent willingness of any group. The key is to NOT ask for an impossible commitment like lifelong friendship, everlasting fidelity, marriage, etc. Remember, the question is "who wants to be with Elaine for a couple of hours over coffee to chat about the possibility of making something happen.

Option II:
An Organized Meeting to Create a Circle..

The second common occasion is when there is an "Elaine", and there is an opportunity to create a gathering of people to sit with her and begin to create/plan a future. "Who should come? Who gets 'invited'?" Elaine is the key. The simplest way to figure this out is to do "Elaine's Circles". Those in the inner circles should be there. In general, more is better - because many people are part of Elaine's life. Thus, family, friends, work mates, etc. are essential. Teachers, social workers, medical professionals are welcome - but the critical criterion is "who loves this Elaine!". Who is there (potentially) for the long haul. If Elaine has trouble deciding on her own, those she trusts make a list with her - and she can signal yes and no.

Thus, as the circles begin, the facilitator must ensure that the intimate and close supporters are heard clearly. Competent, caring - but more distant professionals with very important talents may well be supportive - but they are unlikely to become intimate friends. Their input (unless they make that kind of personal commitment) should be limited. (There is no expectation that professionals can or should "be friends" with all people they work with. It is not reasonable or possible) Friends, family, colleagues are the key support people who surround Elaine and shape her daily reality. This first gathering may well be simply to listen, but it is also the same type of grouping that is required for a MAP or a PATH. If only one person can come, start there. It is a first step.

We have begun! The *dance of possibility* has started. Ten years down the road, Elaine may have a network, may have a friend. If we do nothing, we know for sure nothing will occur. If we do something, something might happen. No guarantees.

Think about your own relationships. Where did they start? How do they start? Relationships usually begin around common interests, doing things together, friends in common, or having a cup of tea together. This is the place to start.

The criticism we hear is that this is all contrived and manipulated. We choose to say that this work, like life itself, is **intentional** and **invitational**. We believe that without intention and invitation, people live lives of quiet desperation and loneliness. We choose to be in action and to believe that the community will respond to its citizens in need **if asked**. Without the invitation, which is often not only intentional, but even assertive, nothing will happen. People will drown in loneliness while swimming in a world full of possibility and people. Some critics might think this is motivated by pity - to help the unfortunate. But in our experience, NONE of us is exempt from loneliness and being disconnected. It is a lifelong quest to have "full circles". Thus, the assumption that this is "for the disabled" is mis-

taken. Circles are good for all of us!

None of this is easy. It is indeed hard work. But we believe the primary job of the adult human service worker of the 21st century is to build the foundation of the circle so that all our citizens can go on to lead full and decent lives where real choices can be made about how we all live our lives.

The key to all this is that the most effective human service workers are themselves connected in the community and have full lives of their own. Their job descriptions must be to build networks of relationships around people "served" in every way possible, and never to create dependency i.e. clients. We must create **interdependence** i.e. **citizens.**

As we do our work around the globe, we find these tools are enthusiastically received by most human service professionals. They like the tools because it gives their jobs clarity. They don't have to love or even like all the people they work with. They do have to serve the best interests of the people. As a fourth circle worker (paid) they can indeed become a second circle friend. The important issue is to clarify which role (relationship) is dominant and when - contract worker or friend. This is not a value judgment (good or bad), but is vital to ensure safety and to minimize hurt. Paid workers cannot be best friends to everyone, and the "illusion" is very damaging. In one recent situation, two people formerly employee and employer became marriage partners. The new and radiant bride began as an attendant to her groom and has now become his very best friend and confidant. This relationship did not begin with intimacy - it was an "exchange:. However, in organizing the filling of the 3rd circle, they discovered that they were friends - then lovers.

We believe all this is possible if we break out of the old mold and step into the new.

*"Life is either a daring adventure
or nothing at all."*
Helen Keller

MAPS and PATH

MAPS and PATH are two other tools developed and written about extensively by Jack Pearpoint, Marsha Forest, John O'Brien and Judith Snow. They come under the broad category of Person Centered Planning (see Everyday Lives: The Contribution of Person Centered Planning. John O'Brien and Herbert Lovett, Pennsylvania Office of Mental Retardation, Harrisburg, Pennsylvania.) Personal Futures Planning refers to a family of approaches to organizing and guiding community change in alliance with people with disabilities and their families and friends. Each approach to person centered planning has distinctive practices, but all share a common foundation of beliefs.

a. The person is the focus of the planning.

b. The aim of the planning is to change common patterns of community life.

c. In order to support the kinds of changes to improve people's lives virtually all existing human service policies and agencies will have to change the way they regard people and relate to communities.

d. Honest person centered planning can only come from respect for the dignity and completeness of the focus person.

e. Assisting people to define and pursue a positive and possible future tests one's clarity, commitment and courage.

f. Those who treat MAPS and PATH as simply another technique and those who fail to provide for their own development and support will offer little benefit to the people they plan with.

MAPS

MAPs is an 8 step process which gathers information and then utilizes that portfolio of information to develop a plan of action for a person or organization. It is based on **dreaming** and **listening**. The aim of a MAP is to move away from a person's or organization's nightmares and to do everything possible to move towards their dreams. There are training videos and articles dealing with MAPS. Seeing the process in action is critical to using it well. (Video references at the end of the article.)

The MAPS questions are outlined in the circular diagram called the MAPS Mandala. (see diagram). All eight questions must be asked. The process has two phases. Part I of the MAP deals with the history (story) of the person (or organization), their dreams and their nightmares. When doing a MAP, this phase takes approximately half the time (one hour in a two hour MAP)

Part II deals with "*Who is this person? What are his/her unique strengths and gifts? What do we all need to do to avoid the nightmare and reach the dream? What is our plan of action*? We also need to be very intentional and decide when we meet again.

Our cardinal rule of facilitation is that a person must not do a MAP on another human being without first doing several MAPS on oneself. People all over the world are "doing MAPS to others" without ever having experienced the intense vulnerability of the process for their own lives. We cannot enforce or police this, but we can set it down as a point of ethics - human service workers must practice the facilitation and the process on themselves first. We are always stunned by glib assumptions that we can use powerful tools by just reading an article or attending a one day event. We beg human service professionals to be humble in dealing with human fragility. The facilitators we trust are constantly honing their skills on their own lives. They are listeners and dreamers and constant life-long learners.

We would all be outraged if a person announced that they were going to practice "family therapy" after reading an article by a noted family therapist. Yet, we unleash people on other human beings (who are acutely vulnerable) with MAPS and PATH tools, when they have never even read an article or seen a video on the

The MAPS Mandala

Introductions: Who is present? What is their relationship to the person?

What is the Story? History?

What is the Dream?

What is a MAP?

What is the Nightmare?

What is the Plan of Action to avoid the Nightmare and to make the Dream come true?

Who is the Person? *brain storm*

What are the Person's Needs? What do We need to do to Meet these Needs?

What is the Person Good at... strengths, gifts, talents?

JACK PEARPOINT

© Inclusion Press 1992

process. "It is incredible chutzpah (a Yiddish word that means more than nerve!) It is also irresponsible. John McKnight's article "Do No Harm" should be a hallmark for anything we do! (<u>THE CARELESS SOCIETY</u> by John McKnight is published by Basic Books, 10 East 53rd Street, New York, New York 10022-5299 page 101-114)

We therefore urge the readers of this chapter to study the materials, watch the videos and practice, practice, practice. We want people to use these and all other useful tools to support people. But, surgeons study for years, scrub up and use careful protocols to minimize the risk of infection and maximize the possibility of success. We need to be careful too. Take risks - but calculated "viable" risks.

PATH

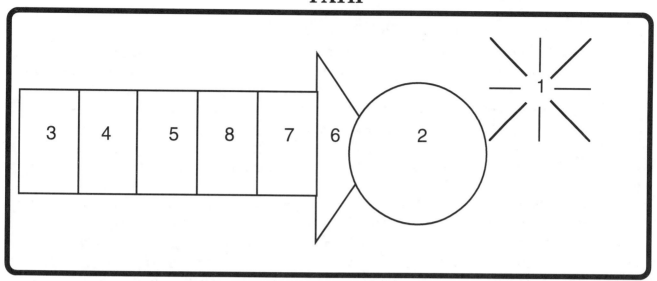

The eight steps in PATH are:

1. Touching the DREAM - "the North Star"
2. Sensing the GOAL.
3. Grounding in the NOW.
4. Identifying people to ENROLL.
5. Recognizing ways to BUILD STRENGTH.
6. Charting Action for the NEXT FEW MONTHS.
7. Planning the NEXT MONTH'S Work.
8. Committing to the FIRST STEP.

PATH

PATH is an even sharper edged than MAPS. A series of 8 structured questions that must be asked **in the order** in which they were designed. At the conclusion of a PATH, a detailed plan of action emerges for the individual or group. PATH was designed to take over when a MAP was not quite enough, or when a situation or organization is more complex. There are excellent training videos and a workbook that explains PATH in detail. Readers need to seek out these materials for further study. (see the PATH Workbook and Path Training Video from Inclusion Press, Toronto).

PATH is one of a family of tools for dealing with complex problems. It is "action learning" in turbulent environments. Eight steps define the PATH process. Their sequence guides Path-finders to clarify the meaning of their work, visualize the results of significant change, experience the tension between where they are now and where they want to be, and outline positive actions to move toward the results they want.

The NORTH STAR

The North Star is the key to the outcome of the PATH process. What we find is that people have a hard time suspending the NOW and really getting into the future. The more we can encourage dreaming and develop a vibrant and colourful North Star, the more the process flows into the positive possible future, the goal section and ultimately, designs first steps into the future.

We have done PATH with individuals, families, small and large organizations. It never fails to be a powerful tool to get people unstuck and into action. Beware the facilitator who feels that the North Star leads people to be "unrealistic." Facilitators must believe that "dreams are dreams" and must NEVER be blocked.

If one understands the process, one sees that after steps one and two (North Star dreaming and the Goal Section) we bring people back to the NOW. But first, we need almost an hour to take people on that journey into the future.

Judith Snow Dreams

Judith Snow, one of our dearest colleagues and friends, has a wonderful story about the North Star. Judith is a major disability rights activist in North America and Europe. Her story of growing up with a physical disability, her subsequent institutionalization and escape from confinement, have served to teach and inspire thousands over the years.

For decades, Judith hid a recurrent fantasy she had as a child and teenager. Her fantasy was that she was a truck driver. Her truck was super high tech - one of those huge more-than-eighteen-wheelers that had a bed in the back, so you didn't have to stop at a motel. You just pull over and sleep.

The purpose of Judith's truck was to drive from Toronto to California, filled with important cargo. She would earn lots of money for this work. She'd work 6 months and make enough money to take off for the other six months. In those six months, she would rest, write, reflect and have fun. Judith reflects, *"I used to be embarrassed about this fantasy because obviously I am not going to be a truck driver. I can drive my wheelchair with my thumb and my mouth, but until the software improves, even I wouldn't want to drive one of those trucks. Of course, when I was small, everyone told me that all the time. But over the years I met many people labeled mentally handicapped who also didn't use words and they began to teach me that they could really communicate with other people even though they weren't using words. I began to look to see where this communication was coming from.*

Finally, I got over the embarrassment about my dream and began to tell it to other people. I have a very strong support circle (my Joshua Committee) and they listened quite seriously. What we all figured out was that my dream, i.e.. my North Star, had all the important seeds of my life in it.

The seeds are that my work is very important to me, that I wanted to get around more, and in fact, I wanted to get all around North America as part of my work. (Now I want to get around the whole world and my North Star is more of a white Lear jet plane). I want to bring something to people I believe is very important. I want to make enough money by doing my work that I can spend time at home resting, reflecting and learning other new things to bring to the world. I am living my dream today!"

Common elements of MAPS and PATH

Both MAPS and PATH are creative facilitated personal futures planning processes. Both are co-facilitated and both have a large graphic as the centerpiece. People ask us if the graphic is necessary. The answer is YES!. Without a graphic and without the key questions, these tools are not MAPS and PATH. (They may be as good and useful, but they should not be called a MAP or a PATH).

The MAP is exploratory, it gathers information and organizes it around the person or organization. A good facilitator will relax the group, demystify the process and take people on an exciting adventure called their life. A MAP is simply a way to get a person or organization where they want to go.

Framework Ground Rules for MAPS and PATH

A MAP or PATH will not work when people don't feel **safe**. We have developed a framework to help set a tone before we begin. Our MAPs and PATH preparation ground rules involve:

1. **Throw away luggage or garbage** before starting. Each participant is asked to write down (if they can) what might stop/block them from really participating or "being present". This can be as complex as being angry at your executive director for the past ten years, or as simple as having had a fight with your son before you came to the meeting.

2. **Take off judging wigs** for at least the length of the MAP or PATH. We must create a place where true listening can take place without judging. (Judging skills are necessary, but like many tools, aren't useful for every problem, and lose their strength if they are turned on constantly.)

3. **Time commitment.** We check people's beepers at the door, and make sure the phones are off. We will not do a MAP or PATH without at least a two hour commitment. This is done publicly and taken very seriously.

4. **Negotiate End Time at the beginning.** After everyone is settled, and we are agreed to spend say 2 hours, we reclarify the END time. If people cannot stay, we decide (at the beginning) whether the PATH or MAP needs to be rescheduled, or if we can adjust the time, or continue. No surprises. (This is not a "guilt trip".) Rather, if we are going to respect a person, we need to confirm attendance. We do not trivialize people's integrity lightly.

5. **All information is shared publicly**. Behind the back murmuring and side conversations are not permitted. By setting these parameters BEFORE the MAP or PATH begins, people can be "coached" to follow the guidelines without feeling attacked.

6. **No MAP or PATH is ever done for a person who is not present.** A parent cannot do a MAP or PATH **for** their son/daughter. We don't do MAPs or PATH ABOUT others. However, we can do a MAP or PATH for the parent and their relationship with their son/daughter. We can PATH how **we** would support a person. This apparently subtle difference is very important.

7. **No jargon!** No terms or initials (i.e. MR, DD, EMR, BD) are used that cannot be understood by everyone. Speak in plain ordinary language or explain words that others may not understand.

One RULE, Three Guidelines
for MAPS and PATH

The one rule is the Golden Rule. Don't ask anyone to do what you yourself are unwilling to do. This keeps everyone honest and on track.

Guideline #1. Ask all the questions as they are outlined in the MAPS Mandala and PATH workbook. In a MAP, the facilitator can be creative in the ordering of the questions, but not in leaving any question out. In PATH, the facilitator must follow the order set out in the PATH arrow.

Guideline #2. Use a graphic. This is a large sheet of paper posted to the wall. The group sits facing the graphic. The graphic should be colourful, using words and images. It is not the artistic quality of the graphic that is important, but the spirit it communicates. Bright colour is important. Only write down what is actually said, not what a facilitator interprets as being said. The facilitator summarizes but does not interpret.

Guideline #3. Use a team to facilitate i.e. two people. One role we call a **process facilitator** (team manager), the second is the **graphic recorder**. This models the teamwork the two tools have at their heart. We say over and over "**You can't do it alone**." We believe team facilitation is a valve in MAPS and PATH.

Ending MAPS and PATH: Get Concluding Words/Images
In a recent MAP with a person moving into supported employment, here is what the group had to say at the conclusion:

Peg: This has been really good for me because its really focused me in a way that most case conferences don't do. This MAP focused on what is really important and what we need to do next.

Edna: I am amazed at how clear everything got. We have real direction now. We also heard the real story not simply what was in the file.

George: I feel it is really complete. We all listened to one another for the first time in years. It was hard to dream and really hard to face the nightmare but after that it got real easy. It was great.

All: We have a real way forward.

The Essence of MAPS and PATH

In facilitating MAPS and PATH, we must have human service workers who listen with ears that don't say *"This is unrealistic, this could never come true."* We need facilitators who listen with their whole hearts and souls and know that in the seed of the North Star is the real story of the person's dream. This is true for an organization as well. The themes of life emerge if the facilitator elicits a North Star that is true. This must be done creatively. The facilitator can use music, props, different lighting, etc. - to give "permission" to dream. The key is to take the time to listen. Create an "empty space" and wait for the dreamer to fill it.

We have watched novice facilitators inadvertently kill the North Star or stifle the dream by their posture, body language, a look in their eye. The PATH may get completed, but it will not be true.

A true North Star takes a facilitator who can call forth the dream, who can wait for it to emerge. The problem is anxious facilitators who over-facilitate rather than waiting and drawing out the North Star. Having the person or team physically touch the paper is also useful. Having them sit near the North Star part of the arrow is key. DO WHAT IT TAKES TO GET THE NORTH STAR. **Facilitators who have never done this for themselves cannot do it for others.**

The problem with most traditional planning tools around vulnerable people (either physically or mentally challenged) is that we focus continually on what is wrong with "them" and their families. We end up trying to fix them. We get stuck. *"You can't fix me,"* Judith says. *"I can't walk. But I can get a great wheel chair and I can surely get into a Lear jet and travel the globe!"*

We have attempted to give readers a glimpse into three exciting tools that we use with individuals and organizations all over the world. They are creative and colorful, but best of all they have helped us in our own lives. We have seen these tools take countless others into territories that once seemed impossible. These tools have nothing to do with disability. They can be used by people in this field, but many others are using CIRCLES, MAPS and PATHS in fields as diverse as small business, Aids and other health related work, family conflict resolution, classrooms and schools, aboriginal community work, etc.

These tools are basically for people who want change. They are not the only tools on the block. They are simply three tools we are proud to have developed and improved over the years. We cannot and will not be the CIRCLE, MAPS & PATH Police. But we do ask you to use them with deep respect and integrity. A tool can create a work of art or be an instrument of destruction. The outcome depends on your skill and integrity.

We are dealing with vulnerable and precious lives. We know readers of this chapter will want to learn more. We invite you to call upon our good friends in New Zealand, Ray Murray and Tricia O'Brien, who are skilled and trusted facilitators of these processes. We also invite you to fax, e-mail, or visit us on our WEB page (http://inclusion.com). Write us with your comments, thoughts and suggestions.

Your first step

You now know what to do. Your first step, if you haven't done so before, is to gather a group of your own friends and family in a comfortable and safe place and do your Circles, MAPS and PATH. If you have done it before, do it again, and again. The more you dream your dreams, design your North Star, state your nightmares (quickly), the stronger you will be. If you can look at who you are, face your gifts and talents, the better you will be to walk with others on the journey we call life.

**The best and most beautiful things in the world
cannot be seen or touched...
but are felt in the heart."
(Helen Keller)**

*The best to you on your journey.
Marsha and Jack*

Reference List: (evolving)

Books:
Path Workbook - 2nd Edition: Pearpoint, O'Brien & Forest   Inclusion Press., Toronto, 1995
What's Really Worth Doing. Judith Snow, Inclusion Press, Toronto, 1994
From Behind the Piano. Jack Pearpoint, Inclusion Press, Toronto, 1992
The Inclusion Papers. Pearpoint & Forest, Inclusion Press, Toronto, 1993
Action for Inclusion: O'Brien, Forest with Snow, Pearpoint and Hasbury, Inclusion Press, Toronto, 1989
All My Life's a Circle: Falvey, Forest, Pearpoint & Rosenberg, Inclusion Press, Toronto, 1994

Videos:
Inclusion: All Means All: An Introduction to Circles, MAPS & Path: Video Journal 1994
Path Training Video: An Introduction to Path: Inclusion Press   1994
Maps Training Video - Shafik's Map, Inclusion Press, Toronto, 1995
With A Little Help From Our Friends - Inclusion Press, Toronto, 1990
Kids Belong Together - from Inclusion Press, Toronto, 1989
Miller's Map - from Inclusion Press, Toronto, 1993

PUTTING ALL KIDS ON THE MAP

Marsha Forest and Jack C. Pearpoint

"Dream your dream," the facilitator urges, and students, families, and friends respond by suggesting many ways to bring almost any child into the regular classroom. This teamwork approach to planning enables educators to end the segregation of special education students.

Annie, Tommy, Jay, Andreas, Katherine, Becky, Erica, Mark, Greg, Miller, Peter... the list is too long and too painful to finish.

These are the names of some of the children who have been rejected by public schools in Canada and the United States. They are black and white, girls and boys, youngsters and teenagers.

In common is their parents' simple dream of having their children accepted and educated in a quality school alongside their peers.

In common is the label *disabled* pinned on them, like the yellow star pinned on people labeled Jewish, and the pink triangle pinned on people labeled homosexual, during World War II.

The Nuremberg Trials confirmed to the world that pinning yellow stars and pink triangles on people was a crime against humanity. But today, no trials have ruled that IQ scores and disability labels often sentence children to lifelong failure.

We know that special education is neither special nor educational in any sense of the word. The outcome for people labeled *disabled* is often a life of loneliness, poverty, and joblessness—not an outcome any parents would choose for their son or daughter.

Everywhere we go, people are talking about the "Butwhatabout Kids." Some of the popular euphemisms include *hard to serve* and *at risk*. Why don't we just admit it outright? These are children and teenagers who scare us to death; they make us vulnerable and nervous. That is natural, normal, and human. What is unnatural, abnormal, and inhuman is our systematic "boxing" and subsequent rejection of the people we fear.

When we meet teachers who fear having certain students in their classrooms, we offer alternatives. MAPS (Making Action Plans) is one of those tools that takes responsibility from one person and puts it in the hands of a team that comprises school personnel, family, friends, and the children themselves. (We describe a second practice, Circle of Friends, in "Portrait of Diane" and "Portrait of Norman."

It is glib to think that anyone will learn all he or she needs to know about dealing with children with complex needs in one article. But, with consistent use of MAPS (and Circle of Friends), we have found great success in being able to include almost all children in regular classrooms.

The MAPS Setting

MAPS is a collaborative process that brings the key actors in a child's life together to create an action plan to be implemented in a regular classroom setting. It is not a case conference or an individual education plan (IEP), but the results can certainly be used on any IEP form.

MAPS is facilitated by two people. School personnel or an external team can act as facilitators, and they need not be familiar with the student or the family. However, they must know the MAPS process inside out, and they must believe 150 percent that full inclusion is possible for all. The facilitators must also be good listeners—able to hear great pain without providing immediate advice and solutions. Their main task is to pull information from the group and move it along into an action plan.

One facilitator acts as the "host." This person welcomes the group, explains the process, and guides the questions.

The second facilitator is the recorder, creating a record of what the group says with color and graphics on large chart paper. This public record is an essential element of a MAP

A personal and informal atmosphere is also essential. Before the meeting, the facilitators should set up comfortable chairs in a semicircle. The chart paper and clean markers should be ready along with snacks and colorful name tags.

Eight Key Questions

A MAP is created through eight questions. Each question must be used, but there is no particular order. The facilitators decide on the order depending on the needs of the group. To illustrate how a MAP works, we'll discuss a student named Mark.

Before the questions begin, the facilitator should ask, "Who are you and what is your relationship to Mark?" This sets the collaborative tone for the meeting as participants introduce themselves.

Question 1: What is a map?" Participants are asked to think of the characteristics of a map. One recent group answered:
"A map shows direction."
"It tells you how to get from one place to another."
"It shows you how to find stuff."
"A map tells you where to go."

The facilitator can then explain:

"That's exactly what were here to do: to show direction for Mark's life, to help him and his family get from one place (the segregated class) to another place (the regular class)."

"The MAP will also help us figure out how to find the 'stuff' that Mark needs. If we all work together, we can decide where to go next. Together we can create a plan of action that we can put into practice for Mark starting right away.

Question 2: What is the story? The facilitator can pose this question something like this:

"Please tell us your story. What are the most important things that have happened since Mark was born? I know you can go on and on with this, so I'll limit you to 5-7 minutes. Tell us what you feel is really important for all of us to hear and to know about Mark's story."

The facilitator must listen with heart, soul, and body and be careful not to make this a case history. The facilitator must also ask the participants to listen with their hearts:

"Don't listen just with your ears. Listen with your whole body. Don't be judgmental. This is not a trial. Try to feel and hear what the person is telling you as if it were your own story."

We usually ask this question before the dream question, depending on the mood of the group. The recorder represents the story using words and pictures. The recorder also summarizes the story after the family or student has spoken, checking the facts and essential elements of the story.

(Making simple errors, especially with names, can be very upsetting to people, so request assistance.)

Question 3: What is your dream? This is really the heart and soul of the MAP. The facilitator must create an atmosphere that helps the family and student feel comfortable about sharing their true dreams, hopes, and wants.

The question might be posed like this:

"If you could dream the dream you really want, if you could have anything with no holds barred, what do you really truly want for yourselves and for Mark? Money is no object. Don't hold back. Let yourselves be free. Don't ask for what you think you can get This is different. This is what you really want and dream about or pray for."

There is often a deathly silence at this moment. It is essential. Do not interrupt. Wait. Allow people time to build up their courage to express their feelings and hopes. If this is rushed, the whole MAP may be futile.

When a facilitator asks this question with an honest heart, profound things often happen. In our years of asking this question, parents all over the continent have told us that the MAP empowered them to dream again.

"But," someone out there is thinking. "Butwhatabout" the student who can't speak? We have done many MAPS with children labeled *nonverbal*. Although these children don't speak, they certainly communicate. And if the group knows the child well, someone will be able to articulate his or her own dreams for the child and also the dreams he or she thinks the child might have. For example: "If Mark could speak, what do you think his dream would be?"

Families often weep as they tell us, "My dream is that my child be happy, be included in school, walk or ride to school with his sister, be invited to birthday parties, have a hamburger with a friend, and have the phone ring just for him."

One 12-year-old girl told us, "I want a trip to Hawaii and a job with computers. Also a pet dog." She was clear as a bell!

One parent of a medically fragile child told us, "I want my child to have one real friend before she dies. My nightmare is that my child will never know friendship." (This little girl did die soon after, but because she had moved into a district that welcomed her, the mother did get her wish. The entire 3rd grade class attended her daughter's funeral.)

Question 4: What is my our nightmare? Many people consider the nightmare question the hardest to ask, and we agree. But we believe it is one of the most important because the MAP must identify the nightmare in order to avoid it. Unless the outcome of the plan of action is to prevent the worst from happening, we're just doing busywork.

In 10 years of doing MAPS, we find these are the most consistent responses to the question: "My nightmare is that my child will end up in an institution with no one to love him (or her)." "We will die, and my child will be alone and put in a group home." "My child will never have a friend."

No one has ever said "I'm afraid my child will not get an A in math or learn phonics."

No one has ever said, "I'm afraid there won't be a proper functional curriculum."

This question often breaks the ice between warring factions. A Kentucky woman broke down describing how her 18-year-old son was currently living out his nightmare, being institutionalized, after having blinded himself. "Our family is in the nightmare," she wept. "All we wanted, all we want now, is some shred of human kindness and friendship for our son."

We had to stop for coffee as all participants, both factions, were in tears. For the first time they were meeting as human beings rather than as warriors on opposing sides of a placement review table.

Questions 1 through 4 are Part I of a MAP. It is often necessary to take a break at this point. The second part is lighter, faster-paced, and moves toward the action plan.

MAPS—Part II

Question 5: Who is Mark? This is a brainstorming question. To get started, we like to draw an outline of a person on the chart paper. We hand out sticky notes and ask each person to write one word or phrase that describes the student. We post the notes on the chart paper to give us a snapshot of the student. Mark's snapshot read: *curious, handsome, determined, likes good snacks, always hungry, potential, my son, dimples, pretty ordinary, my brother, very active, pest, a little brat, somebody's great friend someday, an interesting boy, lively, likes to play with drums, great family.*

We sometimes ask, "What have other people said about Mark in the past? What words have been used before in other meetings?" Mark had been described as: *retarded, developmentally delayed, autistic, severely autistic.* These words should be posted separately, but the recorder may want to highlight the dramatic differences between the two portraits of the same person.

Question 6: What are Mark's strengths, talents, and unique gifts? What is he good at? Another list is generated: *happy beautiful boy, loving, friendly, he can look you in the eye and smile, gives a lot, he has a "look," helps to put things in perspective, makes you feel good.*

This brainstormed list is important as it gives us many ideas for the curriculum and daily program: Mark likes to throw balls, play with ropes and strings, climb in parks, eat, relax, swim laps in the pool, play in water puddles, go skating, play in clothes closets, and be with people.

By this point we have generated an enormous volume of information on Mark, and it's time to move to an action plan.

Question 7: What does Mark need? What do we need to do to meet these needs? At this MAP the only people present were Mark's mom, dad, teenage sister, and a dedicated teacher/friend. When it came to Mark's needs, there was a real consensus that Mark "needs to be involved and to meet people his own age." The family needed him to meet other children so his mother could begin to build a life of her own.

Question 8: What is the plan of action to avoid the nightmare and to make the dream come true? The family agreed that it would be a godsend to find someone to take Mark to local places where he could get involved with other kids. The job description for that person was developed from what was said at the MAP:

- Find places where he can meet kids.
- Find kids to spend time with him.
- Go to the youth center.
- Get involved in trips, swimming, and activities.
- Develop more communication skills.

When you frame the needs question carefully, it flows directly into an action plan. When planning a curriculum, for example, we might draw the timetable and have the other students brainstorm all the activities that Mark likes and could do. Then we would explore the logistics. If

Mark is going to get from history to gym and be dressed in 10 minutes, he will need help - a guide. Who would be willing to help? We link specific people to specific times, places, classes, activities. A concrete action plan, with actual activities to do right away, is crucial. (An additional planning tool, called PATH, uses the information gathered in the MAP to develop a strategic plan of action.)

In this instance, the family enthusiastically agreed to plan a pizza party and invite some neighborhood kids—that weekend. Together with Greg, the teacher/friend, they started to look for someone to take Mark into the community. Greg agreed to facilitate another MAP with a wider group in one month.

As the MAP is concluded, the recorder talks the group through a summary of the charts and presents them to the family as a gift. Other tokens, such as a plant or a cake, are also presented.

Before the meeting ends, the facilitator asks each participant one more question:
"Will you give me one word, or a phrase, to sum up your experience of this MAP. Off the top of your head, the first thing that springs to mind..."

Mark's group answered:

Mom: "I'm relieved. Great session."
Dad: "Very positive. Thanks."
Mark: (gives us all a really big smile)
Greg: "Fabulous and positive."

A Kaleidoscope

The MAP is like a kaleidoscope, a mysterious and magical toy that changes constantly. Through the eyepiece we see little bits of beautiful color and light turning together in an everchanging mosaic.

The kaleidoscope picture is like the outcome of each MAP: people work together to make something unique and better happen. The MAP is more than anyone can do alone. It proves what we strongly believe—
together we're better!

Portrait of Diane

Try to imagine a world in which you do not have a single person who truly loves you. Imagine that you see only paid personnel in the morning and at bedtime. Imagine a world where none of your peers speaks or walks. Imagine having no family and no friends.

Recently, we met a young woman who literally had no one in her life. She is 16 and knows no one her own age. Diane had been abandoned by her parents at 4 and placed in a group home for children with severe to profound mental retardation.

As we did her MAP, Diane sat with us and listened intensely to the conversation. We were told that she banged her head and screamed constantly. The Diane we observed sat still for two hours and listened intently. What did she hear? What did she understand? It is our belief that she heard and felt our concern. We believe she responded to that caring by sitting with us for two hours.

It was clear that an intentional Circle of Friends needed to be built immediately. Diane had spent her days in a segregated class in a regular high school. Though she was at the school, no one really knew her.

The school called together a group of teenagers and teachers who expressed an interest in helping Diane.

"How would you feel if your life was like Diane's?" we asked.

One young woman said without hesitation, "I'd commit suicide." Others said, "I'd sleep all the time." "I'd take drugs." "I'd drink." "I'd kill someone."

They saw immediately that what Diane needed most was to be with them—to get out of the segregated room. They brainstormed places they could go with Diane. There was a rock concert coming up, and one student volunteered to take Diane with her and her other friends. Another decided to visit Diane and have dinner with her at the group home. The students thought Diane would like the music and cooking classes with their noise and "pretty cool" teachers. The ideas flew. Diane sat through the meeting with a smile as she gently rocked back and forth, back and forth.

Several teachers decided to get involved. Rather than blaming themselves for what they had done in the past, they switched their energy into actions they could deliver in the future.

The result: Diane now has regular visitors to her group home. She has gone out more in 6 months than in the past 10 years, and one teacher and student seem to have formed a special bond with her. They have invited Diane to their homes for dinner and to go on Sunday outings. Best of all, Diane is out of the segregated room and goes to music, cooking, and other regular classes. She hangs out in the lunch room and has stopped poking the corners of her eyes and screaming as much as before. Is Diane "cured"? No! Does she now have people to talk to, things to do, a life to look forward to? Yes!

Equally important, Diane's classmates are getting hands-on experience in problem solving (number one issue in the curriculum) with a real and relevant problem. They have to create curriculum and timetables and troubleshoot with Diane. They are learning to manage teachers, manage behavior, and confront values. Their friendship with Diane may be one of the most important learning activities of their lives. And now Diane has a dream, with a new Circle of Friends as a part of it.

Portrait of Norman

Norman wanted to go to camp, but everywhere he and his family went, they were told that Norman's needs were too great. One young counselor wrote us this letter illustrating the simplicity and complexity of the idea of a Circle of Friends.

We decided Norman could attend our camp. That was a big step in the right direction. I had all the kids together in the recreation hall, and I gave my little speech. "A circle of friends is any support group that helps any camper having problems feel more welcome and included." I was received with blank stares.

After bombing with this great opening statement, I simply asked the kids to talk about Norman, who they had met that morning. "What do you think Norman can do all day at camp?" Boom! Everyone was talking at once. That was a question 10-year-olds could relate to. It wasn't a lecture on circles.

The meeting lasted about 20 minutes, ending with suggestions about how they could do things together with Norman. I asked for a smaller group of volunteers to help me plan Norman's day. *Everyone volunteered.*

Norman's biggest challenge and the reason he had been rejected by every other camp in the universe was "weak bladder control." Several people (adults) had suggested that Norman should sleep in a separate building to "hide" the problem.

I decided (with Norman's permission of course) to put the issue out in the open. The children suggested (quite matter-of-factly) that they take turns waking Norman up in the night to go to the bathroom. It never occurred to them (and they rejected outright) the suggestion that he sleep in another building! The counselors volunteered to take turns helping when needed.

Many baseball games, slumber parties, canoe and splashing trips later, Norman no longer requires a 'one-to-one' worker. His bladder problems are getting better (only twice a week instead of every night). Norman's circle of supporters (now a smaller group of real potential friends) meets for an hour every four days. The children and counselors really look forward to it. So does Norman. Norman's circle has become a place for all involved to get support. Last week Norman wasn't even the issue. The topic of the day was Tanya's bad temper.

Finally I should tell you that the social worker called me in shock regarding the progress Norman had made. She asked if we could work on building a circle in his school and in his group home community this fall. I told her I would love to come and help one of the school people become a facilitator. I guess I really learned a lot in the workshop on MAPS and Circles. Norman was my chance to try it out myself. It was the best experience of my career. I'm launched.

Thanks and love, Dan

As Norman's story illustrates, attitudes are the major barrier to including all students in all activities. But attitudes are no longer an adequate excuse. We must welcome all children now. It is their right.

INCLUSION PRESS INTERNATIONAL
ORDER FORM

24 Thome Crescent
Toronto, ON   Canada M6H 2S5
Tel 416-658-5363 Fax 416-658-5067
E-mail: 74640.1124@compuserve.com
WEB PAGE: http://inclusion.com

Classic Videos

With a Little Help From My Friends
Prod: M. Forest & G. Flynn
The basics of creating schools where all kids belong and learn together. Hands on strategies – MAPS & Circles of Friends.

Kids Belong Together
Prod: People First Assoc of Lethbridge, Alta Featuring the late Fr. Patrick Mackan – a celebration of friendship – MAPS in action.

Together We're Better
Producer: Comforty Media Concepts
Staff Development Kit: a 2 hour video 3-pack of resources with Marsha Forest, Jack Pearpoint and Judith Snow demonstrating MAPS, PATH and CIRCLES. An inspiration.

Miller's MAP
Prod: Expectations Unltd &Inclusion Press
Children, parents, neighbors and professionals make inclusion happen– team facilitation and graphics in a MAP.

Friends of ...Clubs
Producers: Oregon Dept. of Education & University of Oregon A beautiful 15 min. story about creating community partnerships. Friends, friends, friends - the spark of life.

Dream Catchers
Producer: Institute on Disability, NH
New 16 minute video about dreams and circles of friends. Beautiful images, personal stories, images of the future. An inspiration.

PATH DEMONSTRATION Video
Producer: U. of Dayton, Inclusion Press
60 minute Path with a group of educators and parents. An excellent demonstration of Path problem solving in action with a team.

Inclusion News
The Center publishes an independent annual newspaper - articles & resources you need . It has raving fans! International flair. Order in volume - $50 for a box of 150. A Conference Must!

Inclusion Exclusion Poster
by Jack Pearpoint
A vibrant eye catching 18" X 24" graphic poster exploring the why behind Inclusion and Exclusion.

Courses for your consideration...

New Videos! New Videos!

NEW WHEN SPIDER WEBS UNITE
Shafik in Action
Prod: Inclusion Press & Parashoot (35 min)
Shafik Asante - edited from Toronto Summer Inst, July, 1996. An inspirational talk on community and inclusion. A tribute to a friend/colleague - includes slide show on Shafik.

NEW CHANGING the SYSTEM
Follow the Yellowknife PATH
Prod: Inclusion Press & Yellowknife Educ. Dist.1
An incredible 3 days with administrators, faculty and students planning the future of an entire school system. PATH and other creative tools demonstrate leadership and vision in action.

NEW ALL MEANS ALL
the Inclusion Video
Prod: Video Journal & Inclusion Press
An outstanding introduction to Circles, MAPS and PATH. Produced by the Video Journal, this tape is a great beginning - showing all three major tools. (30 min)

NEW Everyone Has a Gift
Building Communities of Capaity
Prod: Inclusion Press & Parashoot (60 min)
A JOHN McKNIGHT Keynote - the opening of the Toronto Summer Institute in July, 1996. McKnight at his finest.

NEW New MAPS Training Video
SHAFIK"S MAP
Prod: Inclusion Press & Parashoot
MAPS- step by step - John O'Brien facilitating Shafik Asante's Map. How to make families partners in planning. Holistic, creative, colorful futures planning for people, families, organizations. + Judith Snow on Dreaming. (45 min)

NEW PATH Training Video
Introduction to Path
Prod: Inclusion Press & Parashoot (35 min)
Exciting, creative, colorful futures planning tool. Jack & Marsha demonstrate 8 steps with an individual and his family. An excellent introduction - linked to the PATH book.

Friendship: It's About Time
Produced by Vision TV, Exec. Prod: Rita Deverell, Prod: Sadia Zaman
27 minute video exploration of friendship: joys, heartaches & maintenance, featuring Marsha, Jack and Judith.

Come to the 3rd Annual
TORONTO Summer Institute
Inclusion, Community & Diversity
July 4-10, 1998

Hosts for the Learning Community:
- John McKnight
- John O'Brien
- Marsha Forest
- Jack Pearpoint
- Judith Snow
- Bahiya Cabral Asante
- Nkosi Ali Asante
- Dave Hinsberger(July 8)

The Creative Facilitator
A four day hands-on course to practice Circles, MAPS, PATH, Solution Circles, Graphic Recording and Process Facilitation
Available in Toronto or on the Road

Tools for Change
A Course that delivers a Tool Box of practical useful ideas to make any organization or family an All Star act - Six Thinking Hats, Team Building, All Star Company, Making Meetings Matter

VIDEO Now Available from Inclusion Press:

INCLUSION: ALL MEANS ALL
an Introduction to
Circles, MAPS and PATH
30 minutes

The perfect companion to this book:
Produced by the Video Journal of Education,
this half hour video is an excellent introduction to the tools
Circles, MAPS and PATH.

INCLUSION PRESS
International

24 Thome Cresc.
Toronto, Ont. M6H 2S5
tel: 416-658-5363 fax: 416-658-5067
e-mail: 74640.1124@compuserve.com
Publishers: Jack Pearpoint & Marsha Forest

Dec. 1997 edition

New Books!   New Books!

Yes! She Knows She's Here
by Nicola Schaefer
The inspiring story of Catherine Schaefer's move from her family home to a home of her own. A story of possibility, change, hope and most of all love. Essential reading and powerful writing for every family - that's all of us. .

INCLUSION: RECENT RESEARCH
by Gary Bunch & Angela Valeo
Outstanding summaries of the research on inclusion in education. Indispensable knowledge base for anyone involved in inclusive education. Libraries, schools, faculties, families...

When Spider Webs Unite
Challenging Articles on Inclusion & Community
NEW!   by Shafik Asante
A collection of articles and essays on community, diversity and inclusion - written by Shafik Asante. Brilliant incisive writing. For anyone who wants to ACT! Read, reflect then 'just do it'.

ALL MY LIFE'S A CIRCLE
NEW Expanded Edition
Using the Tools: Circles, MAPS & PATH
M. Falvey, M. Forest, J. Pearpoint & R. Rosenberg
Introduction to circles, MAPS & PATH - a great place to start!

Members of Each Other
Building Community in Company With People With Developmental Disabilities
John O'Brien & Connie Lyle O'Brien
Remarkable & thought provoking - about building community.

Kids, Disabilities and Regular Classrooms
Annotated Bibliography of Selected Children's Literature on Disability
Gary Owen Bunch
An exciting guide to positive stories about children. An excellent resource for every classroom, family and human service organization.

Petroglyphs
Institute on Disability: Univ. of Hew Hampshire A stunning photo essay on Inclusion in High School. An outstanding book in the UNH series - uncompromising, inspiring narrative - elegant.

The Whole Community Catalogue
editor: D. Wetherow
Indispensable guide for building communities and supporting inclusion. Beautifully organized, chock full of ideas, quotes, resources.

Don't Pass Me By:
Gary Bunch
Writings from "street kids" labelled illiterate: "bad, sad, mad and can't add".

Path: 2nd Edition
5th printing
Planning Possible Positive Futures
Pearpoint, O'Brien, Forest
A guide to exciting, creative, colorful futures planning for families, organizations and schools to build caring "including" places to live, work & learn. Graphics unleash capacity. Path - an eight step problem solving approach involving dreaming and thinking backwards. Color graphic included!

The Inclusion Papers
3rd printing
Strategies to Make Inclusion Happen
Jack Pearpoint & Marsha Forest
Practical, down to earth and sensible. Perfect for conferences, courses and workshops. Circles of Friends, MAPS, articles about drop-outs, kids at risk, Medical School course and more... graphics, poetry, overheads...

What's Really Worth Doing
& How To DO IT! *by Judith Snow* A book for people who love someone labeled disabled - possibly yourself. "This is a book of wisdom – an invitation to the dance of life." John McKnight

TheAll Star Company
Building **People, Performance, Profit** Team
Teams ★★★ *Nick Marsh* ★★★ Building
An exciting book about BUILDING TEAMS and CHANGE. The All Star metaphor is about building powerful teams in your organization.

Action for Inclusion
5th printing
by O'Brien and Forest with Pearpoint, Snow & Hasbury
Over 20,000 copies distributed – "A down to earth blueprint of what 21st century education ought to be doing for all kids in regular classrooms. Modest but powerful strategies for making it happen in a jargon -free, step-by-step book." Herb Lovett, Boston
L'Intégration en Action: Maintenant disponible en Français

From Behind the Piano
3rd printing
Building Judith Snow's Unique Circle of Friends
by Jack Pearpoint afterword: *John O'Brien*
This is the story of Judith Snow & her Joshua committee. It demonstrates that love, determination and hard work will conquer challenges. An inspiration for anyone struggling to make a difference.

Changes in Latitude/Attitude& Treasures
Two books from Inst. on Disability, NH
Changes: The Role of the Inclusion Facilitator - beautifully presented – the experience and wisdom of facilitators in New Hampshire.
Treasures: Photo essay on friendship - images of children in New Hampshire explains how to include everyone. Just do it.

Lessons for Inclusion
Curriculum to Build Caring Elementary Classrooms - Inst. on Disability, U of MN
Step by step - day to day in elementary classrooms. Outstanding collection of curriculum ideas proven in classrooms in Minnesota.

Reflections on Inclusive Education
Patrick Mackan C.R.
Stories and reflections - for your family, assemblies, classrooms, church.

INCLUSION PRESS INTERNATIONAL
ORDER FORM
24 Thome Crescent
Toronto, ON   Canada M6H 2S5
Tel 416-658-5363 Fax 416-658-5067
E-mail: 74640.1124@compuserve.com

WEB PAGE: http://inclusion.com

Classic Videos

With a Little Help From My Friends
Prod: M. Forest & G. Flynn
The basics of creating schools where all kids belong and learn together. Hands on strategies – MAPS & Circles of Friends.

Kids Belong Together
Prod: People First Assoc of Lethbridge, Alta Featuring the late Fr. Patrick Mackan – a celebration of friendship – MAPS in action.

Together We're Better *Video*
Producer: Comforty Media Concepts
Staff Development Kit: a 2 hour video 3-pack of resources with Marsha Forest, Jack Pearpoint and Judith Snow demonstrating MAPS, PATH and CIRCLES. An inspiration.

Miller's MAP *Video*
Prod: Expectations Unltd &Inclusion Press
Children, parents, neighbors and professionals make inclusion happen– team facilitation and graphics in a MAP.

Friends of ...Clubs *Video*
Producers: Oregon Dept. of Education & University of Oregon A beautiful 15 min. story about creating community partnerships. Friends, friends, friends - the spark of life.

Dream Catchers *Video*
Producer: Institute on Disability, NH
New 16 minute video about dreams and circles of friends. Beautiful images, personal stories, images of the future. An inspiration.

PATH DEMONSTRATION Video
Producer: U. of Dayton, Inclusion Press
60 minute Path with a group of educators and parents. An excellent demonstration of Path problem solving in action with a team.

Inclusion News
The Center publishes an independent annual newspaper - articles & resources you need . It has raving fans! International flair. Order in volume - $50 for a box of 150. A Conference Must!

Inclusion Exclusion Poster
by Jack Pearpoint
A vibrant eye catching 18" X 24" graphic poster exploring the why behind Inclusion and Exclusion.

New Videos! New Videos!

NEW WHEN SPIDER WEBS UNITE
Shafik in Action
Video
Prod: Inclusion Press & Parashoot (35 min)
Shafik Asante - edited from Toronto Summer Inst, July, 1996. An inspirational talk on community and inclusion. A tribute to a friend/colleague - includes slide show on Shafik.

NEW CHANGING the SYSTEM
Follow the Yellowknife PATH
Video
Prod: Inclusion Press & Yellowknife Educ. Dist.1
An incredible 3 days with administrators, faculty and students planning the future of an entire school system. PATH and other creative tools demonstrate leadership and vision in action.

NEW ALL MEANS ALL
the Inclusion Video
Video
Prod: Video Journal & Inclusion Press
An outstanding introduction to Circles, MAPS and PATH. Produced by the Video Journal, this tape is a great beginning - showing all three major tools. (30 min)

NEW Everyone Has a Gift
Building Communities of Capacity
Video
Prod: Inclusion Press & Parashoot (60 min)
A JOHN McKNIGHT Keynote - the opening of the Toronto Summer Institute in July, 1996. McKnight at his finest.

NEW New MAPS Training Video
SHAFIK"S MAP
Video
Prod: Inclusion Press & Parashoot
MAPS- step by step - John O'Brien facilitating Shafik Asante's Map. How to make families partners in planning. Holistic, creative, colorful futures planning for people, families, organizations. + Judith Snow on Dreaming. (45 min)

NEW PATH Training Video
Introduction to Path
Video
Prod: Inclusion Press & Parashoot (35 min)
Exciting, creative, colorful futures planning tool. Jack & Marsha demonstrate 8 steps with an individual and his family. An excellent introduction - linked to the PATH book.

Friendship: It's About Time
Video
Produced by Vision TV, Exec. Prod: Rita Deverell, Prod: Sadia Zaman
27 minute video exploration of friendship: joys, heartaches & maintenance, featuring Marsha, Jack and Judith.

Courses for your consideration...

Come to the 3rd Annual
TORONTO Summer Institute
Inclusion, Community & Diversity
July 4-10, 1998
Hosts for the Learning Community:
- John McKnight
- John O'Brien
- Marsha Forest
- Jack Pearpoint
- Judith Snow
- Bahiya Cabral Asante
- Nkosi Ali Asante
- Dave Hinsberger(July 8)

The Creative Facilitator
A four day hands-on course to practice Circles, MAPS, PATH, Solution Circles, Graphic Recording and Process Facilitation
Available in Toronto or on the Road

Tools for Change
A Course that delivers a Tool Box of practical useful ideas to make any organization or family an All Star act - Six Thinking Hats, Team Building, All Star Company, Making Meetings Matter

Books

		Copies	Total
Path Workbook - 2nd Edition	$15 + $5 /1st copy shipping*	____	____
Planning Positive Possible Futures			
All My Life's a Circle	$15 + $5 /1st copy shipping*	____	____
New Expanded Edition- Circles, MAPS & PATH in Action			
When Spider Webs Unite	$15 + $5 /1st copy shipping*	____	____
Challenging Articles on Community & Inclusion by Shafik Asante			
Members of Each Other	$15 + $5 /1st copy shipping*	____	____
Collected Articles on Building Community & Friendship - O'Brien&Lyle O'Brien			
Yes! She Knows She's Here	$15 + $5 /1st copy shipping*	____	____
Nicola Schaefer's NEW Book			
Inclusion: Recent Research	$20 + $5 /1st copy shipping*	____	____
What the Research Says - G. Bunch & A. Valeo			
The All Star Company	$25 + $5 /1st copy shipping	____	____
It's About Building Teams!			
Lessons for Inclusion	$15 + $5 /1st copy shipping	____	____
Curriculum Ideas for Inclusion in Elementary Schools			
Kids, Disabilities & Regular Classrooms	$15 + $5 /1st copy shipping	____	____
Annotated Bibliography of Children's Literature on Disability			
What's Really Worth Doing	$12 + $5 /1st copy shipping	____	____
Judith Snow's new Book on Circles			
The Inclusion Papers - Strategies & Stories	$15 + $5 /1st copy shipping	____	____
The Careless Society - John McKnight	$20 + $5 /1st copy shipping	____	____
Who Cares - David Schwartz	$20 + $5 /1st copy shipping	____	____
Changes in Latitudes/Attitudes	$15 + $5 /1st copy shipping	____	____
Petroglyphs - the High School book from UNH	$15 + $5 /1st copy shipping	____	____
Treasures	$15 + $5 /1st copy shipping	____	____
Reflections on Inclusive Education	$12 + $5 /1st copy shipping	____	____
Don't Pass Me By	$12 + $5 /1st copy shipping	____	____
Action for Inclusion Classic on Inclusion	$15 + $5 /1st copy shipping	____	____
Parcours: Path en francais	$15 + $5 /1st copy shipping	____	____
L'Intégration en Action (en Français)	$15 + $5 /1st copy shipping	____	____
From Behind the Piano	$12 + $5 /1st copy shipping	____	____
The Whole Community Catalogue	$15 + $5 /1st copy shipping	____	____
Inclusion – Exclusion Poster (18 X 24)	$10 + $5 /1st copy shipping	____	____
Inclusion News (free with book order)	$2 + $2 for shipping	____	____
Inclusion News in Bulk (box of 150)	$50 – includes shipping in NA	____	____
Path KIT - 2 Videos + Workbook	$115 + $10 shipping per kit	____	____

Videos

		Copies	Total
* **CHANGING the SYSTEM**	$100 + $8 shipping /1st copy*	____	____
Follow the Yellowknife PATH			
* **ALL Means ALL - Inclusion Video**	$100 + $8 shipping /1st copy*	____	____
An Introduction to Circles, MAPS and PATH			
* **When Spider Webs Unite - Video**	$75 + $8 /1st copy shipping*	____	____
Shafik Asante in Action - Edited Video Talks on Inclusion & Community (30 min)			
* **EVERYONE Has a GIFT**	$75 + $8 shipping /1st copy*	____	____
John McKnight Keynote - Building Communities of Capacity			
* **NEW MAPS TRAINING Video**	$75 + $8 shipping /1st copy	____	____
Shafik's Map - step by step			
* **PATH TRAINING Video**	$75 + $8 shipping /1st copy	____	____
Path: Introductory Training Video			
PATH Demonstration Video (# 2)	$55 + $8 shipping /1st copy	____	____
Follows PATH Training Video			
NEW FRIENDSHIP VIDEO	$55 + $8 shipping /1st copy	____	____
Judith, Marsha & Jack on friendship			
Dream Catchers (Dreams & Circles)	$55 + $8 shipping /1st copy	____	____
Friends of ... Clubs -Friends, friends, friends	$55 + $8 shipping /1st copy	____	____
Interdependence Teenagers Exploring	$55 + $8 shipping /1st copy	____	____
Miller's MAP - MAPS in Action	$55 + $8 shipping /1st copy	____	____
With a Little Help from My Friends	$55 + $8 shipping /1st copy	____	____
The Classic on Circles & MAPS			
Kids Belong Together MAPS & Circles	$55 + $8 shipping /1st copy	____	____
Together We're Better (3 videos)	$175 + $12 shipping	____	____
Staff Development Kit			

GRAND TOTAL $==========

* Shipping: Books: $5 for 1st+ $2/copy up to 10; Videos: $8 for 1st+ $4/copy up to 5. BULK Rate: 15%

Name: _____
Organization: _____
Address: _____
City: _____
Prov./State _____
Work Phone _____
Home Phone _____

Post Code/ZIP _____
Cheque Enclosed _____
Fax _____

INCLUSION PRESS ORDER FORM

24 Thorne Crescent, Toronto, ON
Canada M6H 2S5
Tel 416-658-5363 Fax 416-658-5067
e-mail: 74640.1124@compuserve.com
WEB Page: http://inclusion.com

About the Authors:

Mary A. Falvey,
Professor of Special Education
California State University, Los Angeles
5151 State University Dr.
Los Angeles, CA. 90032   (213) 343-4400

Marsha Forest,
Director of Education
Centre for Integrated Education and Community
24 Thome Crescent
Toronto, Ontario
Canada M6H 2S5   (416) 658-5363

Jack Pearpoint,
Executive Director
Centre for Integrated Education and Community
24 Thome Crescent
Toronto, Ontario
Canada M6H 2S5   (416) 658-5363

Richard L. Rosenberg,
Career Assessment & Placement Center
Vocational and Training Coordinator
Whittier Union High School District
9401 South Painter Ave.
Whittier, CA. 90605   (310) 698-8121

Inclusion Press
appreciates the support of
Imperial Oil Limited

Esso Kids Program

Imperial Oil